Harvard Business Review

ON

MERGERS AND
ACQUISITIONS

THE HARVARD BUSINESS REVIEW PAPERBACK SERIES

The series is designed to bring today's managers and professionals the fundamental information they need to stay competitive in a fast-moving world. From the preeminent thinkers whose work has defined an entire field to the rising stars who will redefine the way we think about business, here are the leading minds and landmark ideas that have established the *Harvard Business Review* as required reading for ambitious businesspeople in organizations around the globe.

Other books in the series:

Harvard Business Review Interviews with CEOs

Harvard Business Review on Brand Management

Harvard Business Review on Breakthrough Thinking

Harvard Business Review on Business and the Environment

Harvard Business Review on the Business Value of IT

Harvard Business Review on Change

Harvard Business Review on Corporate Governance

Harvard Business Review on Corporate Strategy

Harvard Business Review on Crisis Management

Harvard Business Review on Decision Making

Harvard Business Review on Effective Communication

Harvard Business Review on Entrepreneurship

Harvard Business Review on Finding and Keeping the Best People

Harvard Business Review on Knowledge Management

Harvard Business Review on Leadership

Harvard Business Review on Managing High-Tech Industries

Harvard Business Review on Managing People

Harvard Business Review on Managing Uncertainty

Other books in the series (continued):

Harvard Business Review

ON

MERGERS AND ACQUISITIONS

A HARVARD BUSINESS REVIEW PAPERBACK

The *Harvard Business Review* articles in this collection are available as individual reprints. Discounts apply to quantity purchases. For information and ordering, please contact Customer Service, Harvard Business School Publishing, Boston, MA 02163. Telephone: (617) 496-1449, 8 A.M. to 6 P.M. Eastern Time, Monday through Friday. Fax: (617) 496-1029, 24 hours a day. E-mail: custserv@hbsp.harvard.edu

Library of Congress Cataloging-in-Publication Data
Harvard business review on mergers and acquisitions.
     p. cm. — (Harvard business review paperback series)
    Includes index.
    ISBN 1-57851-555-6 (alk. paper)
    1. Consolidation and merger of corporations.   I. Title: On mergers and acquisitions. II. Title: Mergers and acquisitions.   III. Harvard business review. IV. Series.
HD2746.5 .H373 2001
658.1´6—dc21   00-052989
                                  CIP

Contents

Harvard Business Review

ON

MERGERS AND
ACQUISITIONS

Lessons from Master Acquirers

A CEO Roundtable on Making Mergers Succeed

MODERATED BY DENNIS CAREY

Executive Summary

THE ANNOUNCEMENT IN JANUARY of the merger between America Online and Time Warner marked the convergence of the two most important business trends of the last five years—the rise of the Internet and the resurgence of mergers and acquisitions. M&A activity is at a fever pitch, spurred in large part by the breathtaking influx of capital into the Internet space. And all signs indicate the trend will only accelerate.

Against this background, an impressive group of experienced deal makers came together to share their experiences of what makes mergers work. They were assembled in Scottsdale, Arizona, under the auspices of the M&A Group, a professional society formed in 1999 for CEOs interested in M&A as a business strategy. Participants included top executives from Internet start-ups like Teligent; venture capital firms like Baroda Ventures;

1

financial institutions like Merrill Lynch and Pricewater-houseCoopers; and major corporations like Allstate, Tyco International, SmithKline Beecham, Rohm and Haas, VF, Crown Cork & Seal, and Hughes Space and Communications.

The spirited and surprisingly frank discussion cut a wide swath, considering issues such as whether most mergers fail to pan out as well as expected, how to increase the odds of success, the nuts and bolts of the integration process, the trade-offs between acquiring a company and growing from within, the importance of cultural issues, and why anyone would want to be on the board of a merged company. For roundtable participant bios, see the end of this article.

The announcement in January of the merger between America Online and Time Warner marked the convergence of the two most important business trends of the last five years: the rise of the Internet and the resurgence of mergers and acquisitions. M&A activity has been at a fever pitch recently, and all signs point to an even further acceleration of deal making, spurred in large part by the breathtaking influx of capital into the Internet space. Many executives will be placing bets on M&A that will put their companies' futures at stake.

We at HBR are very pleased, therefore, to share with our readers a lively discussion of M&A and its role in the new economy by a group of chief executives who all have deep experience in making deals work. In a roundtable held last December at a meeting of the M&A Group in Scottsdale, Arizona, these executives addressed a number of important and timely topics, including the trade-offs between acquiring a company and growing organically, the changing shape of M&A strategy, and the keys to successful integration.

The Editors

Dennis Carey: *I'm sure some of you are familiar with studies suggesting that most mergers and acquisitions do not pan out as well as expected. Has that been your experience? Are mergers and acquisitions worth it?*

Alex Mandl: I would take issue with the idea that most mergers end up being failures. I know there are studies from the 1970s and '80s that will tell you that. But when I look at many companies today—particularly new-economy companies like Cisco and WorldCom—I have a hard time dismissing the strategic power of M&A.

In the last three years, growth through acquisition has been a critical part of the success of many companies operating in the new economy. In fact, I would say that M&A has been the single most important factor in building up their market capitalization. I remember that when I bought McCaw Cellular for AT&T back in 1993, everybody said we'd paid too much. But with hindsight, it's clear that cellular telephony was a critical asset for the telecommunications business, and it would have been a tough proposition to build that business from

> *"In the last three years, growth through acquisition has been a critical part of the success of many companies operating in the new economy. In fact, I would say that M&A has been the single most important factor in building up their market capitalization."*
> *—Alex Mandl*

scratch. Buying McCaw was very much the right thing to do. The plain fact is that acquiring is much faster than building. And speed—speed to market, speed to positioning, speed to becoming a viable company—is absolutely essential in the new economy.

David Bohnett: I agree with Alex. For some Internet companies in particular, M&A is certainly the fastest way to expand and solidify their businesses. That was one of the driving reasons behind our decision to sell GeoCities to Yahoo! in 1999. The two companies had compatible cultures and a similar vision of how the Internet was evolving. But the real reason we came together was that it was a fast way for both of us to continue to build competitive mass and expand our user base.

Ed Liddy: I'm not sure that it's so black and white. Acquisitions are certainly a very good way to add a product line or distribution channel that would be too costly to build from scratch. But they don't replace internal growth or alliances. In my business, as in many of today's knowledge industries, assets go up the elevator in the morning and down again at night. They can walk out the door if they feel disfranchised. The build or buy decision therefore becomes a bit more delicate. I usually like to build internally when I feel confident that we have the product and process knowledge to capitalize on an opportunity quickly. Only if we don't have that knowledge, and if we see a company that provides a good strategic fit, will we go the buy route.

David Komansky: You don't want to fall into the trap of making acquisitions just for the sake of it. Although we've made over 20 acquisitions at Merrill Lynch in the last decade as we've expanded—including a $6 billion purchase of Mercury Asset Management—we didn't set out to make them. We started out with what we considered to be a well-forged, highly tuned strategy and decided between acquisitions and green-field investments depending on which approach we felt would more quickly fulfill our ambitions. And we've had our ups and downs in both situations.

Ed Liddy: I'd just like to say one more thing about the bad rap on M&A. I think one of the reasons for it is that acquisitions are so visible. When they fail, they draw intense notice. But a lot of things in business fail; we've all started projects that didn't work out. The internal failures simply don't get as much attention.

Dennis Carey: *The obvious follow-up questions are, How do you raise the odds of success? How do you choose the right companies to buy or merge with?*

Dennis Kozlowski: Tyco has been very aggressive in making acquisitions. The key thing I've learned is that acquisitions work best when the main rationale is cost reduction. You can nearly always achieve them because you can see up front what they are. You can define, measure, and capture them. But there's more risk with revenue enhancements; they're much more difficult to implement.

Unfortunately, people are often too optimistic about revenues. One of the businesses we're in, for example, is medical products. I've seen a lot of health care businesses think that, just by virtue of having more products, they'll be able to sell more to hospitals or other medical service providers a lot quicker. But it takes a long time to train salespeople to bundle the new products with their existing ones effectively and have them accepted in the market. For one thing, the salespeople have to deal with new competitors—the people already selling the same kinds of products they've just added to their bundle.

Jan Leschly: I'm not sure I'd go along with that entirely. Of course, I'm more famous for the deals I didn't make than for the ones I did! But when we at SmithKline Beecham look at acquisitions, we do focus on revenues because our production costs, once we've developed a drug, are minimal. So if we can increase revenues, we're in great shape. And what really drives revenues in the drug business is R&D; there are enormous opportunities in the new technologies now being developed. When we looked at merging with Glaxo, for example, we were talking about synergies in R&D. By merging the two organizations, we probably could save in the neighborhood of $500 million. That's $500 million more a year we could reinvest in the R&D itself, and that's where the merger's real benefit would be.

In terms of improving growth, though, I'd have to say that we have been much more successful at acquiring products and technologies than at acquiring companies. We have a venture capital fund that invests in start-up biotechnology companies whose products and services we then buy. We invest small amounts—half a million dollars here and a million there—and we put our people on the boards. Once the companies get going, we can decide whether to buy them out completely or not. With large acquisitions, you're buying an awful lot of problems along with the products and technology they bring. Our venture capital investments, though, grow with us, and we can see exactly how they might fit in.

Raj Gupta: Obviously, acquisitions can add value in many ways, and you need to gear your M&A strategy to the needs of your company and the realities of your industry. In the chemical industry, where Rohm and Haas operates, much of the M&A activity is driven by the industry's need to consolidate. Currently, there are more than 200 chemical companies with more than a half-billion dollars in sales. As one analyst put it, a large specialty-chemical company is an oxymoron. With this degree of fragmentation, there's certainly plenty of scope for cutting costs through acquisitions. But cost reduction shouldn't be the sole goal; the most successful companies will be those that can grow, as well. When we make acquisitions, therefore, our real aim is to create larger platforms for growth. When we bought Morton, the chemical and salt company, we knew we could make significant gains on two fronts. First, we were able to strengthen our technology base by tapping into Morton's expertise in polyurethane adhesives and powder coatings. Second, we were able to bring Rohm and Haas's considerable access to new geographic markets to the Morton portfolio.

Jan Leschly: But acquisitions aren't always a workable way to get into a new geographic market. We've been struggling for the last ten years with how best to build a business in Japan, for example. From a cultural perspective, it would be very difficult for us to acquire a company there. And the Japanese distribution system is so fragmented that we can't feasibly establish a direct presence. So we're trying to find other ways to do business—alliances, joint ventures, and so on.

Dennis Carey: *Looking at the deals we're seeing these days, it seems there's been a shift from buying companies outside your business space to buying ones within your business space. Is that the key to success?*

Mackey McDonald: We certainly view it like that. At VF Corporation, we focus on the core businesses that we know—like jeans and intimate apparel—and we try to bring our core competencies to acquisitions in those areas. An acquisition becomes attractive if it offers us a new consumer segment or geographic market to sell our products to or if it adds new products to one of our core categories. In our business, we find that if we venture too far from our core competencies, the risk isn't worth it. Many of the companies we buy are run by entrepreneurs who generally know a lot more about why they're selling than we know about why they're selling. We like to stick to our core businesses so if we run into problems, we have the resources and know-how to resolve them.

Jan Leschly: That's true for us as well. Not so long ago, the pharmaceutical companies were on an expansion kick. They spread into cosmetics, then got into consumer products, and finally into service businesses. In our case, we've been successful as a pharmaceutical company and as a major consumer health care company. But when we expanded into service businesses, we soon found that service provision is just not one of our core capabilities. We are a company based on innovation. We're good at manufacturing and systems.

Dennis Kozlowski: I've worked at companies that did diversify outside their core businesses, and I can tell you that they were never very successful. They'd take profits from good, established businesses and put the money into the next high technology. But they usually didn't have the management talent to support the new products or the services that they were investing in. Diversification was the main reason for company failures in the 1960s, '70s, and even the '80s. You can come up with quite a list of companies—think of Hanson PLC, ITT, and SCM—that had good ideas and then spoiled them by going out to invest in the next hot business. In contrast, companies that are doing well today are very focused. At Tyco, we have the same core businesses as a $27 billion company that we had when we were just a $200 million company.

Dennis Carey: *Alex, you said earlier that M&A was a critical strategic tool for growth in the new economy. Can you expand on that for us?*

Alex Mandl: As I said before, the need for speed forces companies to acquire rather than build. The smart Internet and communications companies, for example, are using their high market caps as currency to buy companies and quickly solidify their positions as the new economy takes shape. Take WorldCom. Five years ago, I don't think anybody around this table had heard of it. Thanks to a series of rapid and clever acquisitions, it's now one of the top two telecom companies in the world.

No one knows for sure where we're all going to end up. But we know that we need to get there quickly. You need to carve out your space. And the only way to do that is through acquisitions. The pace, in the telecom world at least, is furious, and it's not going to let up until we know who the major players in the broadband world are going to be.

Jan Leschly: Using acquisitions to expand into the Internet space is a much less obvious strategy for those of us who aren't already Internet businesses. A company like SmithKline Beecham faces huge challenges in figuring out what to do with the Internet. Before we can even think about acquisitions, we need to understand the implications of the Net for our business. I really think that when it comes to the Internet, SmithKline Beecham has a leadership crisis. At least, that's the sense I'm trying to create in our organization. I have to make people at the top understand that we have very little knowledge of how to work in the new market space. The people who really understand it are very low in our hierarchy. They have no responsibility, no authority, no money. We're getting into a situation where it's the young people who have to mentor us—not the other way around. That's a huge problem for middle and upper management to realize, and they're understandably reluctant to delegate too much authority to younger people.

David Bohnett: I agree that it's usually very difficult for traditional companies to integrate Internet start-ups. Traditional companies' processes, cultures, and business models don't work in the new economy. In fact, most successful Internet businesses have evolved on their own, relying purely on the commercial possibilities of the Internet. The huge amount of money out there for Internet start-ups, of course, has made it easy for them to do that.

Mackey McDonald: Jan's point reflects our experience in the apparel business as well. In building up our Internet capabilities at VF, we quickly found out that you can't just go buy technology companies. They have a whole different mind-set than apparel companies do, a different pace. It's easier to figure out how to do business in Japan than in the new technology culture. We've found that the best solution is to form partnerships with independent companies. That's what we are doing with 12 technologies in the business-to-business arena. Also, we can't lose sight of the fact that our business is still heavily dependent on traditional retail channels, and we think a lot more apparel will continue to be sold in stores, not on-line. So when you announce that you're going to compete with your customers—the retailers—and sell direct to consumers, you're bound to run into problems. You don't want to undermine 98% of the business for the sake of a 2% opportunity.

Dennis Carey: *David, you've been working hard to bring Merrill Lynch into the Internet space. Why did you decide to build rather than acquire?*

David Komansky: There was great debate within the firm about that. We could certainly have acquired almost any of the on-line brokerage firms if we had chosen to, and there were those within our organization who wanted to. But we didn't feel that it was the right course. After all, one of the great challenges facing e-companies is building an image and a brand. If you watch TV now, you'll be swamped with e-commerce companies advertising their wares. For us, though, the Merrill Lynch brand is probably our greatest asset. So our strategy is to leverage our name and move the battleground away from price and technology by offering much the same price structures as the leading on-line brokers. In our business, technology is going to be a sine qua non, so everyone in the game will have it. But if we can force the game to content, it will be very difficult for other on-line competitors to match what we can provide.

> *"Adjusting to the new economy is like trying to change the tires on a 747 in the middle of landing. Something is going to get squeezed somewhere."*
> —David Komansky

It's certainly been a very, very difficult trip for our organization. Adjusting to the new economy is like trying to change the tires on a 747 in the middle of landing. Something is going to get squeezed somewhere. It took us a long time to get over our denial and accept the fact that the Internet is not a temporary phenomenon but a true change in the marketplace. It had reached the point where we had earned the reputation of being Luddites. Now that's all changed. We recognize that a certain segment of our clientele wants to deal in the virtual environment. Either we provide that opportunity for them or they go over to companies like Schwab.

We still have a lot of work to do in teaching our sales force how to deal with the pricing pressures that the Internet is putting on our business, and the challenges of managing our core businesses along with the Internet are very trying. But I do think that the emotional transition is well behind us.

Dennis Carey: *Let's pick up on that thought and turn to some of the softer issues surrounding M&A. We often hear about deals collapsing because of cultural incompatibilities. What's been your experience with cultural integration issues?*

Jan Leschly: It's a necessary condition for any deal that there be a good rationale for integrating the businesses. But, in my experience, even if the rationale for a deal is terrific, the deal can still fall apart because of cultural differences. Merging a U.S. and a European company, as we have done, is a particularly complicated process. The management styles are totally different. People have different views on how to manage a global organization. Where should management be centralized, and where should it be decentralized? How should you pay people? The British and American philosophies are so far apart on those subjects they're almost impossible to reconcile.

Dennis Kozlowski: I'm not so sure that culture is as important as it's made out to be. I've never seen a deal really fall apart on a culture issue—or any soft issue. Most collapse on price, one way or another, and managers just use soft issues as an excuse. I accept that companies do have different cultures and that reconciling them can be a lot of work for both sides. But I've been able to live with different cultures and adjust to them.

Bill Avery: Well, having just acquired a European company, I can tell you that there is one cultural difference still very fresh in my mind. Let's say you're not making your budgets because the selling prices of your products are falling. In the U.S., we'd think, "Well, if prices are going down, we've got to cut costs." But in Europe, some managers may be inclined to say, "Well, prices are falling now, but in a couple of years, they'll go back up." My experience at Crown has been that European management tends to be generally less aggressive in cutting costs than we are here in the U.S., perhaps because margins traditionally have been higher in Europe. That's a really big culture clash.

At Crown Cork, we think we are very, very good at cost control, so we are working hard to get a more consistent style across the company. In fact, in the packaging industry, our profits are the highest in our categories. When you buy a company outside the U.S. as we did, you really need to know what you're getting into, and that's hard to get at in due diligence.

David Komansky: It's totally futile to impose a U.S.-centric culture on a global organization. We think of our business as a broad road. All we expect people to do is stay on the road within the bounds of our strategy and our principles of doing business. We don't expect them to march down the white line, and, frankly, we don't care too much if they are on the left-hand side of the road or the right-hand side of the road. You need to adapt to local ways of doing things. The only firms in our industry that have been really successful on a global basis are Goldman Sachs, Morgan Stanley, and ourselves. That's because we've been more flexible than investment banks from other countries.

Nicholas Moore: Cultural differences are not just a matter of geography. Different companies can have very different attitudes and ways of working. In merging Price-Waterhouse with Coopers, for example, we've had to put together people who've been competing against each other for 40 years. So culture has been a really big part of the equation. You have to build trust, and that takes a lot of managerial attention and time.

Ed Liddy: It's important to remember that you don't always have to have a high degree of cultural integration. You can't try to slam every acquisition into one mold. In the last 12 to 15 months, we've probably made four or five acquisitions. In some cases, we've completely integrated them into Allstate. But in other cases, much to the chagrin of our very good Allstate executives, I've said, "I don't want you to 'Allstate-ize' them. I want them to be separate." In the end, what you do with an acquisition depends on the channels and the products that you and the acquired company are in.

Dennis Carey: *Let's shift to some of the mechanics of integration. How do you approach it, and what are your priorities?*

Raj Gupta: At the beginning of negotiations, you tend to concentrate more on the business portfolio, but as the deal advances, your focus switches to people and processes. And once the deal closes, you often have to move very quickly on those fronts. The first thing you have to do is settle the uncertainty of who's going to report to whom and who's responsible for what. When we bought Morton, we put the new management team in place just 24 hours after announcing the deal. Doing that helped people to focus externally rather than internally. Losing external focus is one of the biggest risks when you integrate two businesses—and that's when you lose people and customers.

Once you've answered the key people questions, then you have to start integrating the basic work processes, computer systems, financial systems, and so on. You shouldn't underestimate the difficulty here. You'll find that you won't always get the information you need to make a timely decision—especially in the early days. That's why it's essential to have the right people in the right places within your organization—people you can trust to use a solid combination of data evaluation and intuition to make the best and fastest decisions for your organization.

Ed Liddy: When we announce an acquisition, we try to have the management structure completely laid out. I think the work of integration really needs to start when you're planning the acquisition because it's tied up with the whole reason you're buying the company. You have to start asking the right questions early. At Allstate, we have an integration team that works hand-in-hand with our strategic-planning area. They'll press the planners: "What's the logic of this acquisition? Is it cost takeout? If it is, what processes do we have that we can transfer to the acquired company to bring it up to a level of performance that we're comfortable with? What can we borrow from them that would help us?" And we communicate, communicate, communicate. We say the same thing over and over again to the acquired company, to ourselves, to Wall Street. That way, a common understanding of what we're trying to do can emerge.

Mackey McDonald: After an acquisition, you have to face a room full of people who want to know, "What happens to me?" If you don't answer that question, they don't hear much else of the presentation. Obviously, you can't say, "Everyone here is fine, and no changes are going to take place." What we try to do is explain the process that will determine the new management structure. If you can show how that's going to work, it does relieve some of the concerns. You've then got to pull in the smartest people you have to implement the changes. It's particularly important to do this for international acquisitions. When we acquired our Wrangler-licensed business from Mitsubishi in Japan, we came across all the culture issues we've been talking about here. We couldn't put in people who would immediately try to Americanize the company. We had to understand the local culture, or at least be willing to learn about it before making any changes.

"A very interesting statistic I once read says that people are normally productive for about 5-7 hours in an eight-hour business day. But any time a change of control takes place, their productivity falls to less than an hour."
—*Dennis Kozlowski*

Jan Leschly: It's extremely important to reach out to the second tier of management quickly. When we acquired Sterling Drug in 1994, we used a consulting company to evaluate all our managers—not just Sterling's—in every single country in which Sterling operated. They did it in just three weeks. It was a tremendous morale boost for Sterling's managers, who didn't feel that they were just being slaughtered. In fact, we had to fill 87 jobs around the world in the integrated operation, and 57 of them were filled by Sterling's managers.

Dennis Kozlowski: A very interesting statistic I once read says that people are normally productive for about 5.7 hours in an eight-hour business day. But any time a change of control takes place, their productivity falls to less than an hour. That holds true in merger situations. Inevitably, people immediately start thinking about themselves. So moving fast and getting the right people in place are extremely important. At Tyco, we look to the companies we acquire to provide those people. We present our objectives and our philosophy, and we look for the people who respond. Often, it's not the top executives but rather the people under them who are the quickest to understand and embrace the new philosophy.

At one company we acquired, we took a group of about 25 people off to a small town in Germany for a long weekend to consider ways of changing the business. They came up with a drastically different organizational structure for the company, which we implemented pretty well 100%. But more important, the company owned those changes. They weren't forced on it by us— they came from within. The more you can create a culture that encourages actions like that, the greater your chances of success. I might add that it's almost impossible to build such a culture when you do hostile acquisitions, which is why we don't do them.

Dennis Carey: *When there are integration problems, where do they tend to arise?*

Tig Krekel: I've been in companies that have been acquired, and I can tell you that people become extremely sensitive to every announcement, to every detail. Where is headquarters going to be located? How many people are going to lose their jobs? The in-house rumor is 400, but the acquiring company says 200. You need constant communication to avoid paralysis and maintain morale.

Another flash point is the customer. In the drive to complete a deal, it's easy to lose sight of the concerns of customers. There's almost never any detailed analysis in due diligence of how the customers will react or of the pros and cons of the deal from their point of view. But if you're in a noncommodity business with a small number of large customers, as we are at Hughes, you really do need to have a handle on who will control those relationships after the deal. You can't have ambiguity when it comes to customers.

Jan Leschly: It's true that merger talk makes a lot of people unhappy. But it can also make a lot of people very happy, and that brings its own problems. Think of all the people who can say, "My goodness, this gives me the chance to retire a little earlier. I get this wonderful package. My stock options are vested. This is a wonderful opportunity for me to get out of here." The potential for an exodus of talent is very real. And it becomes even more real in hostile takeovers. As we speak, think of what's going on inside Pfizer, Warner-Lambert, and American Home Products—three companies in the midst of a whirlwind of takeover talks and rumors. What do you think is happening in those organizations today? Think of the oppor-

> *"It's true that merger talk makes a lot of people unhappy. But it can also make a lot of people very happy, and that brings its own problems. Think of all the people who can say, 'My goodnesss, this gives me a chance to retire a little earlier.'" —Jan Leschly*

tunities to recruit from them. Whichever deal gets made, a lot of people will just cash in and leave. At SmithKline Beecham, we spend a lot of time figuring out how to retain people who have just become multimillionaires. What incentives can we give them to stay? In any deal, the impact on talent has to be at the top of the agenda.

Dennis Carey: *One of the most delicate questions in any merger or acquisition is the composition of the board. Although good directors are tough to find, not many are being brought in from acquired companies. Why is that?*

Alex Mandl: It depends on whether people have an interest in joining. Most of the time, board members move on to something else. Craig McCaw, for example, declined a seat on the AT&T board because he realized that he was going to start up new businesses, as of course he has.

I think your comment about it being tougher to find board members really begs the question of why, in today's world, you would want to be on a board. Yes, it's an interesting group of people, and it can be an interesting experience. But I'm amazed, frankly, at how much talk there is in mergers about the importance of combining the two boards. Why is it important that both groups end up on the same board? Taking a board role, it seems to me, might make more sense with an exciting new company, where you might have a significant personal stake and where you can truly help get the company going.

Ed Liddy: We've certainly found very good directors through acquisitions. The challenge is finding people who are prepared to represent the interests of all shareholders, not just the management or the shareholders of the company whose board they were originally on. Clearly, you'll always have an affinity for that part of the organization, but you have to move beyond it. I think most people who sit on multiple boards understand that.

Jan Leschly: I have to say that we've never taken on any board members from our acquisitions. It's not a policy; it's just never happened. It's a different story for mergers, though, where board membership can be a very sensitive issue. It's tough to face your board and tell half of them that they're not going to join the new board. It doesn't exactly create an easy atmosphere. Normally, you just combine the two boards as one big one and then over a year or two it comes down to a normal size again. Of course, most mergers are really acquisitions. People called it a merger when Squibb teamed up with Bristol-Myers. I was president of Squibb at the time, and I can assure you that it was certainly not a merger of equals. It was an acquisition, and the majority, by far, of Squibb's management team was dismissed. If it really had been a merger of equals, that couldn't have happened.

Dennis Carey: *And with that, I'd like to bring to a close what I think has been a very productive discussion. Thank you very much.*

The M&A Group

Founded in 1999 by Dennis Carey, along with Jan Leschly and Dennis Kozlowski, the M&A Group calls itself "the club for acquisitive CEOs." The purpose of the group, which currently has 40 members, is to bring together CEOs who are interested in M&A as a business strategy and provide them with a confidential forum to discuss ideas and share experiences. In addition to attending semiannual conferences, members can access information and interact with professional advisory firms at the group's Web site (www.themagroup.com). The principal participants at the M&A Group roundtable were (in order of appearance):

Dennis Carey (Moderator) is a cofounder and currently serves as cochairman of the M&A Group. He is also vice chairman of recruitment consultants Spencer Stuart US, where he jointly heads the company's Boards and M&A Advisory practices.

Chairman and CEO of Teligent since 1996, **Alex Mandl** was previously number two at AT&T, where he was responsible for orchestrating AT&T's takeover of McCaw Cellular. Teligent offers local and long-distance voice, data, and Internet services to small and midsized companies in the United States.

David Bohnett was a cofounder and the CEO of GeoCities, which was purchased in 1999 by Yahoo! for $3.7 billion. Today, he runs an Internet start-up fund called Baroda Ventures and serves on the boards of several companies, including NCR, NetZero, and Stamps.com.

Ed Liddy became the chairman and CEO of Allstate, the insurance company spun off from Sears, in January 1999. Since his appointment, Allstate has made two major acquisitions for a total of $2.2 billion and has also entered into several promising alliances.

David Komansky has been chairman and CEO of Merrill Lynch since 1997. One of America's leading brokerage houses and one of the world's top investment banks, Merrill Lynch has made over 18 acquisitions in the last five years, including the purchase of Mercury Asset Management for $6.6 billion in 1997.

Dennis Kozlowski has been chairman and CEO of Tyco International for eight years. Tyco is a diversified manufacturing and service company with offerings that range from fire and safety systems to underwater telecom systems. In the last two years alone, Tyco has spent about $25 billion on acquisitions, including the purchase of AMP for $12 billion. Kozlowski also serves as cochairman of the M&A Group.

Just retired in April, **Jan Leschly** had been CEO of drug powerhouse SmithKline Beecham for about six years. Shortly after the roundtable, SmithKline Beecham agreed on terms for its long-anticipated merger with Glaxo, a deal valued at about $180 billion.

Raj Gupta has worked at specialty chemical company Rohm and Haas since 1971. He became its chairman and CEO in October 1999. Rohm and

Haas recently completed the acquisition of Morton International, a manufacturer of specialty chemicals and salt, for $4.9 billion.

Mackey McDonald joined VF Corporation in 1983 and became its chairman and CEO in 1996. Founded 100 years ago, VF is a leading apparel manufacturer with sales of $5.5 billion. The company's brands include Lee, Wrangler, Vanity Fair, JanSport, Jantzen, and Healthtex. Recent acquisitions include Penn State Textiles, Fibrotek, Horace Small Holdings, and Todd Uniform.

Bill Avery became CEO of Crown Cork & Seal, a global leader in consumer-goods packaging, in 1989. Since then, the company has made some 19 acquisitions, including the purchase in 1996 of France's CarnaudMetalbox for about $4.5 billion.

Currently chairman of PricewaterhouseCoopers, **Nicholas Moore** was previously the chairman and CEO of Coopers & Lybrand. Trained as a lawyer, he has spent more than 30 years in the accounting and professional services world since first joining Coopers & Lybrand in 1968.

Previously CEO of AlliedSignal's aerospace equipment unit, **Tig Krekel** became president and CEO of Hughes Space and Communications in January 1999. HSC is a subsidiary of Hughes Electronics, itself a unit of General Motors.

Originally published in May–June 2000
Reprint R00312

The Fine Art of Friendly Acquisition

ROBERT J. AIELLO AND
MICHAEL D. WATKINS

Executive Summary

IT'S NO SECRET THAT the track record of corporate acquirers has been dismal. But there is a group that's had consistent success. A recent study on M&A reveals that between 1984 and 1994, fund investors at some 80% of LBO firms enjoyed returns equal to or greater than their cost of capital on their M&A investments. And this was true even though in many cases the prices paid for the companies were pushed up by competing bidders.

Why are financial acquirers so much more successful than their corporate counterparts? It's because they approach the negotiation process differently. Most corporate managers treat acquisitions as a direct-march-up-the-hill kind of exercise: "I want to buy this company. Let's find out what it's worth, offer less, and see if we get it." The actual deal management is delegated to outside experts—investment bankers and lawyers.

But fund investors treat deal management as a core part of their business conducted by a permanent group of experienced executives, and they have well-established processes that they stick to. The authors examine how the best acquirers approach all five stages of deal negotiations—screening potential deals, reaching initial agreement, conducting due diligence, setting final terms, and reaching closure—comparing good practice with bad, to reveal the secrets of their success.

A RECENT STUDY ON M&A turned up a surprising statistic. Between 1984 and 1994, some 80% of LBO firms reported that their fund investors had received a return that matched or exceeded their cost of capital, even though in many cases the prices paid for the companies those funds acquired were pushed up by competing bidders. That figure stands in stark contrast to the overall record of M&A investments, which from the corporate acquirer's perspective has been dismal, at times disastrous.

The fact that financial acquirers are so much more successful than most corporate acquirers may come as a shock to some managers. After all, financial investors don't bring synergies to their acquisitions, and they often have relatively little operational experience in the industries involved. Indeed, it's highly likely that the target's management team will initially view potential acquirers with substantial skepticism.[1]

Why, then, are financial acquirers so successful? Based on our experience advising companies on both acquisitions and negotiation strategy, we believe the answer lies in their approach to the acquisition process. Most corporate managers treat acquisitions as a direct-march-up-the-hill kind of exercise: "I want to buy this company. Let's find out what it's worth, offer less, and see if we get it." The actual deal-management process is often delegated to outside experts—to investment bankers and lawyers.

But senior managers at financial investors—and the more successful corporate acquirers—treat deal management as a core part of their business. They approach potential acquisitions with sensitivity and a well-established process. They adjust their negotiating postures and objectives as the deal evolves. And they take the trouble to carefully coordinate the different actors— senior managers, lawyers, investment bankers, and so on—throughout the process. It is this care and effort that enables successful acquirers to create the value they do.

In this article, we'll describe how successful acquirers manage their deals. Our focus is primarily on friendly deals, but much of what we found is applicable in a hostile context as well because even a hostile bid has to end in an agreement to work together. All friendly M&A deals pass through five distinct stages: screening potential deals, reaching an initial agreement, conducting due diligence, setting the final agreement, and ultimately closing. (See "Managing the Deal Cycle" at the end of this article.) We'll walk you through that process, comparing good practice with bad, and then we'll suggest ways companies can turn their deal-making experiences into organizational learning.

Screening Potential Deals

Acquisition possibilities can pop up without warning and usually need to be evaluated quickly. A core challenge in sizing up potential acquisitions, therefore, is to balance the need to think strategically with the need to react opportunistically. Experienced acquirers follow two simple rules in screening deals.

LOOK AT EVERYTHING

Successful acquirers are always on the lookout for deals. An LBO shop such as the New York City-based Cypress Group might complete only two or three deals a year, but it will have explored as many as 500 possibilities and have closely examined perhaps 25 of them. Successful corporate acquirers do much the same, albeit on a smaller scale. Cisco Systems, for example, typically evaluates three potential markets for each one it decides to enter and then takes a hard look at five to ten candidates for each deal it does. Assessing a large volume of opportunities confers two main benefits. It gives Cisco an overall sense of what kinds of strategic acquisition opportunities exist and at what price, making the company better able to assess the value of each prospect relative to the others. On a more basic level, it forces managers to bring discipline and speed to the screening process.

KEEP A STRATEGIC FOCUS

A common mistake for novice acquirers is to cast strategy aside in the face of an exciting opportunity. "The failure starts right at the beginning," one senior financial professional explained to us. "Someone at the top falls in love, and the word comes down, 'We are going to do that deal.' Once the decision gets made, the guys doing the deal just want to get it done. They start stretching the operating assumptions to make it work." Senior executives at LBO firms, however, are strict about sticking to guidelines. Joe Nolan, a partner at GTCR Golder Rauner, is very clear about his firm's focus: "We look for businesses where acquisition will be a core part of the growth strategy. We back people who know how to both operate and acquire companies, which is a rare combination. We invest in service companies and not manufacturing."

From Talking to Planning

Initial negotiations can take place in a variety of ways. Some cases occur through a structured process, such as an auction; others happen less formally through conversations between senior executives. Either way, the challenge at this second stage is for the senior management of both companies to agree that the potential for a deal is sufficient to justify investing resources in further exploration. Successful friendly acquirers follow much the same rules of thumb in nursing potential transactions through this phase.

DON'T GET BOGGED DOWN OVER PRICE

It is usually unwise to try to establish a firm agreement on price this early. The parties simply don't have enough information. As Bob End, one of the founding partners at Stonington Partners, puts it: "You have to do some preliminary feeling out, but if you focus on price at the beginning, you are setting yourself up for failure. People start staking out positions and end up souring on the deal. I'd rather get some momentum around the business possibilities, to get people nodding their heads."

IDENTIFY MUST-HAVES

Although acquirers cannot afford to get tied up with too much detail at this stage, it is essential to pin down certain issues. Many of these are driven by the acquisition's strategic rationale. GTCR Golder Rauner, for example, focuses on the management team's experience and its incentive structure. Cisco insists that the management of target companies believes in employee ownership. It's also important to clarify the roles that the target's top executives will play in the combined organization: who will be retained, and what will they do? American Home Products' merger with Monsanto foundered, for example, because the two CEOs could not agree on which of them would be number one. Finally, it is essential that the acquirer be comfortable at this stage with any potential liabilities—such as environmental exposures, retiree health-care liabilities, or class action suits—that could materially affect the price of the transaction.

Savvy acquirers use early negotiations to foster a sense that both sides are working together in good faith to arrive at a mutually advantageous transaction.

GET FRIENDLY

It's only natural that the management team of a target company going into preliminary negotiations should feel nervous, even suspicious, of potential new owners. Savvy acquirers use early negotiations to foster a sense that both sides are working together in good faith to arrive at a mutually advantageous transaction. They are flexible and respectful in their negotiations, and they try to help target managers see the career opportunities that could result in the new organization. Says Jeff Hughes, vice chairman of the Cypress Group: "We build relationships with partners. It's how we approach deals from the very beginning, from the first meeting. You can't get a deal done unless you understand what the seller wants. You always have to solve people's problems." It's important to build "relationship capital" early on because it will be needed in the later stages of the deal. (See "Managing the Deal Team" at the end of this article.) As the acquisition moves through due diligence, final agreement, and closure, the acquirer's deal team will inevitably become much more assertive and demanding.

Gearing Up for Negotiations

The next stage, due diligence, is the most time consuming and least creative part of the process: the deal goes from the high romance of partnership to the mundane world of fact checking. Unsurprisingly, the eyes of many senior managers tend to glaze over at the prospect, and they *A deal that dies at* leave the job to business devel- *the due diligence stage* opment staff, line managers, *almost always dies for* accountants, lawyers, and *the right reasons.* bankers. But that boredom is dangerous: acquirers have wiped more value off their market capitalization through failures in due diligence than through lapses in any other part of the deal process. Smart acquirers approach a $1 billion acquisition with the same attention to detail they would apply to investing $1 billion in building a new plant.

TURN OVER ALL THE ROCKS

In the excitement of the moment, the novice acquirer may be distracted from looking too closely at the details. That's a mistake because a deal that dies at the due diligence stage almost always dies for the right reasons. Recently, a prospective buyer was conducting diligence on a rapidly growing development-stage consumer service company with a robust product that dominated its niche. Initial assessments were highly favorable, but a deeper look revealed that the visionary founder had not put in place an adequate financial control system. The target's profitability was illusory, and the buyer abandoned the transaction. Hidden problems of this type are about more than money—they also raise important concerns about the competence, even honesty, of the target's management team.

SIZE UP THE OTHER SIDE

Experienced acquirers use due diligence to deepen their knowledge about—and links with—the target's management. Every such interaction offers acquirers a priceless opportunity to assess people's abilities and personal agendas. Do the target's managers have command of their company's operational details? Do they work well as a team? Are they easily flustered or hostile when challenged? Are they enthused by the transaction, or are they more concerned about their personal futures? In due diligence for a recent media deal, for instance, it became clear to the acquirer that the target's founder and owner had certain priorities and motives for the deal, including a desire for a major role in the combined entity. Using that knowledge, the acquirer was able to structure a deal that satisfied the founder's aspirations to such an extent that he was willing to make significant concessions on price.

FEED DUE DILIGENCE INTO BUSINESS PLANNING

For novice acquirers, the due diligence process is just an information-gathering exercise, a break between initial and final negotiations. They usually do not begin to formulate strategy or build a valuation model until the process is complete. In some cases, different people conduct due diligence and final negotiations. Experienced acquirers, however, link their due diligence closely to business planning. Stonington Partners, for example, puts together a book on each acquisition, covering the investment thesis, the business model, capital structure, a base case valuation, a sensitivity analysis, and third-party due diligence. Stonington also keeps the original deal team involved throughout the process.

Getting to Final Terms

The fourth phase of the deal, in which the management teams of both sides and their advisers conduct negotiations on price and strategy, is the most sensitive. A typical mistake for novice teams at this stage is to come to the table with a large list of outstanding issues, which they then try to resolve in no particular order. The danger of this approach is that talks will get stalled on relatively trivial items, exhausting the hard-won goodwill gained in earlier stages and affording openings for rival bidders. Experienced acquirers are conscious of the need to maintain the momentum of the talks, and they are always aware of external threats.

USE MULTIPLE NEGOTIATION CHANNELS

Senior managers, who may have steered the process to this point, often take the view that their company needs to speak with one clear voice at the negotiating table, and therefore they limit the negotiating team to a few key people. We strongly disagree with this approach.

Successful acquirers usually divide their deal team into two or three separate negotiating groups: managers, lawyers, and perhaps investment bankers.

This division of labor has a number of important benefits. For one, it allows for parallel processing. The legal teams can, for example, make significant progress on the acquisition agreement while the bankers address the terms and structure of the financing. The managers, meanwhile, can focus on strategic and personnel issues, stepping into the other negotiations only to overcome impasses. Negotiating through multiple channels also makes it easier to send informal messages. An acquirer's management team may, for example, insist that the major selling shareholder sign a noncompetition agreement. At the same time, however, without conceding this point, the acquirer's investment banker or lawyer could hold hypothetical conversations about different ways to address the same concern. Finally, negotiation at different levels isolates acrimony. The principals can use the bankers and lawyers to deliver hard messages or to take inflexible positions without poisoning relationships with their counterparts.

CULTIVATE ALTERNATIVES

When an opportunity goes live, some deal managers focus on it to the exclusion of other opportunities. That's a natural instinct given constraints on managers' time. Nevertheless, we believe acquirers should carry on as vigorous a dialogue as possible with alternative targets. The value of understanding your best alternative to negotiated agreement (or BATNA) has been well explored in popular books on negotiation, such as Roger Fisher, William Ury, and Bruce Patton's *Getting to Yes* (Houghton-Mifflin,

1992). Knowing what the alternatives are makes it easier to judge the relative value of the deal at hand and can shift the balance of power between acquirer and target. In a recent acquisition of a telecommunications company, for example, the acquirer was able to announce in the middle of negotiations that it had agreed to buy another, related company, significantly reducing its need for the first target. An acquirer's deal team behaves more confidently when it knows it has a choice—and that confidence gets projected across the table.

ANTICIPATE THE COMPETITION

In most acquisitions, the target has a choice, and negotiations may even be taking place in the context of a structured auction. Before deciding on tactics, therefore, acquirers should assess their advantages and disadvantages relative to other potential bidders. (For a list of the key points to consider when comparing your company with potential competitors, see "Are You the Strongest Acquirer?" at the end of this article.) That assessment should include a calculation of the long-term cost of losing the opportunity to a competitor. In some cases, an acquirer may want to avoid that situation by making a preemptive initial bid. IBM's unsolicited bid for Lotus Development, for example, was made at twice the target's prebid stock price.

In general, however, experienced acquirers avoid such tactics. Indeed, some financial acquirers have a strict policy of not participating in competitive auctions because they're convinced that the winner is often the party that overpaid. For the same reason, many corporate acquirers, like Cisco, also insist that substantive conversations be carried out on an exclusive basis.

Making It Happen

Once the ink on the final agreement has dried, it's easy for managers to think that the deal is done, but a surprising number of deals fall apart between final agreement and closure, the last stage of the process. There are sometimes very good reasons for that to happen—an environmental disaster may happen, some undisclosed liability may become apparent, or some adverse change in the target's competitive position may occur. (For instance, in 1998, Tellab's acquisition of telecom equipment maker Ciena fell apart when Ciena lost two key contracts after the final agreement was reached.) But a lot of deals fail at this point because acquirers do not take the trouble to sell the deal to key stakeholders or because they allow too much time to elapse between agreement and closure.

SELL, SELL, SELL

It's understandably hard for management, at the end of an exhausting negotiation, to shift quickly to the task of enthusiastically selling a deal to stakeholders. But in many cases, the final agreement is the first time investors get to voice their opinion on the deal, and their reactions can torpedo it. Earlier this year IMS Health, a major health care information provider, agreed to merge with TriZetto Group, an Internet health care company. The market reaction was immediate and negative— investors wiped some $2 billion off the companies' combined market capitalization. The press noted at the time that a "lack of details surrounding the deal caused the shake-up in the stocks." A major shareholder subsequently released a letter to the company noting management's "inept" performance on an analyst conference call. The transaction was subsequently restructured as merely a sale of an IMS division to TriZetto.

Smart acquirers, therefore, are swift to follow their final deal agreements with aggressive and carefully planned public relations and investor relations campaigns, often involving professional PR advisers. Full and clear disclosure of the terms and the rationale for the deal is key. As Ammar Hanafi, vice president of business development at Cisco Systems, puts it: "I tend to over-communicate. The Street has to understand the strategy and how the acquisition fits in."

Nor can any corporation afford to neglect its key internal constituencies, as Deutsche Bank's CEO Rolf Breuer learned to his cost earlier this year from Deutsche's failed merger with rival Dresdner Bank. His mixed signals about the future of the combined organization's investment-banking operations outraged investment bankers in both camps, ultimately scuppering a deal that would have created a global force in banking.

MOVE FAST

However aggressively the CEOs and managers have sold the deal, not everyone will be happy with it. The target's line employees in particular will be worried about adapting to a different operating culture. In some cases, they will have legitimate concerns for their job security. At the same time, the target's customers will be wondering whether the acquirer will damage long-established relationships. Savvy acquirers keep the time between signing and closing as short as possible—ideally, to less than three months. They realize that quick closure gives them a better chance of showing the target's employees and customers that the deal will work. As Steve Holtzman, chief business officer at Millennium Pharmaceuticals, expresses it: "Time is your enemy. Once you have the idea, and you are agreed, then get it done. You can't go in and slam the deal together necessarily very quickly; you may need an up-front courting process. But once the courting is done, nail it." What's more, a prompt closure provides a signal to key constituents—including investors—that the acquirer's managers know what they're doing.

Learning from Experience

All too often, the expensive lessons that acquirers learn are forgotten once the deal is over. But LBO shops constantly refine their approach; they treat every deal—even the missed opportunities—as a learning experience. Says GTCR Golder Rauner's Nolan: "If we passed on a deal and it succeeded, we'll revisit why we let it go. If we do something and it doesn't work out the way we expected, we sit down and figure out the lessons learned. We also try to pass those lessons on to the executives we've been working with."

In our experience, it's wise to postpone a detailed analysis of a deal for at least a month—especially if there have been problems. In the aftermath of a failed deal, team members will be disappointed and may well channel their energies into a hunt for blame. With the benefit of further information, though (including the subsequent performance of the target), the lessons should become clearer and may often turn out to be quite different from initial impressions. The first postmortem session should therefore be brief, focusing primarily on setting an agenda and a time for holding the later meeting. And fixing that agenda should not be very difficult to do because, as you can see from "Postmortem Questions," the key issues are fairly obvious, although which questions need to be posed depends on whether or not the deal was a success.

As successful acquirers have found, effective deal management is a source of sustainable competitive advantage, especially in rapidly growing or consolidating industries. Companies that can't close deals and are known to be dysfunctional negotiators will have fewer opportunities and will soon be outgrown by their more acquisitive competitors. Conversely, companies that effectively execute an acquisition strategy can vault to leadership positions in their industries. A case in point is Ispat International, a corporate acquirer that conducts its M&A activities very much as an LBO shop does. Twelve years ago, Ispat was a little-known Indian steel

---

Postmortem Questions

Whether a deal succeeds or fails determines which questions to ask when trying to glean lessons learned. In both cases, the questions are straightforward, but the answers are invaluable.

What to Ask After a Failed Deal	What to Ask After a Successful Deal
• Was missing this acquisition a win or a loss for the company?	• What did we do well in the process?
• If it was a loss, what could we have done differently?	• What problems did we miss and when?
• If it was a win, what did we do well that kept us out of this transaction?	• How can we improve our process to uncover those problems earlier?
• How could we have spotted the flaws earlier and spent less time on this opportunity?	• How does what we bought compare with what we thought we were buying?

company with a single mill in Indonesia. Today, thanks
to a series of well-managed and well-timed acquisitions,
it is one of the world's leading steel companies. (For the
story behind Ispat's success, see "Ispat: A Great Corporate Acquirer" at the end of this article.)

Following the operating principles we've described
will certainly help companies become better acquirers.
And they will become even better if they learn how to
learn. But there will always be some element of art to
deal making. Mastery of the art of acquisition can be
achieved only through experience.

Managing the Deal Team

NO TEAM CAN MAKE a bad deal good, but a bad
team can make a good deal bad. The challenges of
managing a deal team are, in essence, much the same
as those of any large project: how can you bring a large
team with a variety of skills and agendas together to
quickly achieve an objective that not everyone may
agree with? It's a task familiar to any film production
company, and experienced acquirers go about it in
much the same way.

Use the same principal actors

While each deal involves a large total cast, deal teams
at successful organizations such as Cypress and Cisco
always have at their core a small group of people who
have worked together in the past. They are then supple-
mented by inside and outside experts. Having an inner
circle of people who are familiar with one another facili-
tates coordination and communication. It also grants the
team a certain amount of emotional resilience in what

can be an unsettling experience. "We are nine senior professionals, and all of us have worked together for at least a decade," explains Cypress vice chairman Jeff Hughes. "That's long enough that everyone knows it's not personal if a deal gets killed. We all succeed or fail together." All transactions must have a clear leader and, although deal managers often start as a deal's advocate, they must be prepared to kill the deal if necessary.

Explain the plot

Team members have to talk to one another, of course, particularly during due diligence. As obvious as this advice might be, it can often be overlooked even though communication can be encouraged by fairly simple formal means, such as placing the working groups in a bullpen environment. Some of the most experienced acquirers require their teams to conduct daily roundtable discussions, so that everyone can hear the progress, the issues, and the concerns of the rest of the team. The deal managers encourage team members to contribute to these meetings and take care to discourage any hoarding of information.

Managing the Deal Cycle

The negotiation of every deal goes through five distinct phases, and for each phase, experienced serial acquirers strictly adhere to several negotiating principles:

1. Screening Potential Deals

- Look at all potential deals in your market, not just at the deal at hand.

- Don't cast strategy aside in the face of an exciting opportunity.

2. Reaching Initial Agreement

- Don't focus on price yet.
- Identify the details critical to the deal's success.
- Use early negotiations to foster a sense of trust with the target's top executives.

3. Conducting Due Diligence

- Look for the devil in the details.
- Deepen your understanding of the target's operating managers.
- Link due diligence with business planning.

4. Setting Final Terms

- Negotiate on several fronts simultaneously.
- Make sure you have alternatives to this deal.
- Anticipate the competition.

5. Achieving Closure

- Oversell to stakeholders.
- Close quickly after setting final terms.

Are You the Strongest Acquirer?

IN COMPETITIVE BIDDING SITUATIONS, an acquirer should compare its position with its rivals' along the following dimensions:

- ability to realize synergies with the target
- financing capacity
- ability to make quick decisions
- attractiveness of currency, in the case of stock-for-stock acquisitions
- reputation for getting deals done
- reputation for treating target's management with respect and for successfully integrating target's management
- postacquisition performance record

Ispat: A Great Corporate Acquirer

ALTHOUGH THE MAJORITY OF corporate acquirers have a poor track record, a few have successfully pursued long-term acquisition strategies. One such company is steelmaker Ispat International.

Ispat (which is Sanskrit for "steel") is one of the world's largest steel companies. This growth has come almost entirely through a decade-long series of acquisitions, starting with the purchase in 1988 of Trinidad and Tobago's state steel companies, and culminating with the purchase of Unimétal, Tréfileurope, and Société Métallurgique de Révigny from the French steel giant Usinor.

What's interesting about Ispat is that its M&A activities are organized very much like those of an LBO shop. To start with, Ispat's acquisitions are strictly focused. As president and COO Johannes Sittard explains: "While our expertise could be used in other industries, we never go outside our core business. So we understand the candidates and have a clear vision for where they could fit."

Once an opportunity has been selected, Ispat sends a small team to visit the seller. Here Ispat tries to gauge the seller's expectations and see if purchasing the assets makes sense. One of the key must-haves for a transaction to proceed to the next stage is that the target demonstrate that its labor supply and access to electricity are solid.

Ispat's due diligence process, which has been honed over time, focuses not just on gathering facts but, as Sittard observes, "We use due diligence to learn about the people who are running the company and to convince them that joining Ispat is an opportunity for them to grow. These conversations provide information you will never find in a data room."

The company works with the potential acquisition's management to develop a five-year business plan that will not only provide an acceptable return on investment but will also chime with Ispat's overall strategy. Ispat's managers know that they may end up responsible for managing the target, and that helps discourage them from making unrealistic assumptions about its prospects.

Ispat relies on a core team of just 12 to 14 professionals to manage its acquisitions. Based in London, the team's members all have solid operational backgrounds and have worked together since 1991. To support the team, Ispat draws in additional experts from its operating units as needed. The company learns from its experiences. "We are a small team, and acquisitions are much of what we do," Sittard explains, "so postacquisition assessments are a permanent part of our conversations."

Note

1. The study that turned up the surprising statistic was published in a 1996 article in *The McKinsey Quarterly* entitled "Growth Through Acquisitions: A Fresh Look," by P. L. Anslinger and T. E. Copeland.

Originally published in Novemver–December 2000
Reprint R00602

Are You Paying Too Much for That Acquisition?

ROBERT G. ECCLES, KERSTEN L. LANES,
AND THOMAS C. WILSON

Executive Summary

DESPITE 30 YEARS OF EVIDENCE demonstrating that most acquisitions don't create value for the acquiring company, executives continue to make more deals, and bigger deals, every year. There are plenty of reasons why value isn't created, but many times it's simply because the acquiring company paid too much. It's not, however, that acquirers pay too high a price in an absolute sense. Rather, they pay more than the acquisition is worth to them.

What is the optimum price? The authors present a systematic way to arrive at it, involving several distinct concepts of value. In today's market, the purchase price of an acquisition will nearly always be higher than the intrinsic value of the company—the price of its stock before any acquisition intentions are announced. The key is to determine how much of that difference is "synergy value"—the value that will result from improvements made when the companies are combined. This value will accrue to the acquirer's shareholders rather that to the target's shareholders. The more synergy value a particular acquisition can generate, the higher the maximum price an acquirer is justified in paying.

Just as important as correctly calculating the synergy value is having the discipline to walk away from a deal when the numbers don't add up. If returns to shareholders from acquisitions are no better in the next ten years than they've been in the past 30, the authors warn, it will be because companies have failed to create systematic corporate governance processes that put their simple lessons into practice.

Despite 30 years of evidence demonstrating that most acquisitions don't create value for the acquiring company's shareholders, executives continue to make more deals, and bigger deals, every year. Recent research shows that acquisitions in the 1990s have just as poor a record as they did in the 1970s. There are plenty of reasons for this poor performance: irrational exuberance about the strategic importance of the deal, enthusiasm built up during the excitement of negotiations, and weak integration skills, to name a few. Many failures occur, though, simply because the acquiring company paid too much for the acquisition. It wasn't a good deal on the day it was made—and it never will be. A good example is Quaker Oats' acquisition of Snapple. Some industry analysts estimated that the $1.7 billion purchase price was as much as $1 billion too much. The stock price of both companies declined the day the deal was announced. Problems with implementation and a downturn in the market for New Age drinks quickly led to performance problems. Just 28 months later, Quaker sold Snapple to Triarc Companies for less than 20% of what it had paid. Quaker Oats' and Triarc's stock prices went up the day that deal was announced.

How should you think about what to pay for an acquisition? And how should you know when to walk away? In the course of a research project on mergers and acquisitions, we explored those questions with 75 senior executives from 40 companies. All were experienced, skilled acquirers. We learned that there's a systematic way for senior managers to think about pricing acquisitions. We also learned that even experienced acquirers, who should know better, sometimes get too attached to a deal. When that happens, it's essential to have organizational disciplines in place that will rein in the emotion. A combination of analytical rigor and strict process discipline will help senior executives and board members guide their companies toward the right acquisitions at the right price.

No Single, Correct Price

It's tempting to think that the reason so many acquisitions are overpriced is straightforward—just that most deals today are too rich, that executives routinely get caught up in the excitement of the race and offer more than they should. Indeed, that's often the case. But it's not always so simple. In fact, the relationship between the size of the premium and the success of the deal is not linear. Consider the 20 deals listed in "Deals with Low Premiums Often Fail—and Vice Versa." In half the cases, the acquirer paid a low premium, and the total return on investment one year later was negative. In the other half, the acquirer paid a high premium, yet total return one year later was positive.

The question, then, is not whether an acquirer has paid too high a price in an absolute sense. Rather, it's whether an acquirer has paid more than the acquisition was worth to that particular company. What one company can afford will differ from what another company can afford and, more than likely, from the asking price. Ultimately, the key to success in buying another company is knowing the maximum price *you* can pay and then having the discipline not to pay a penny more.

Ultimately, the key to success in buying another company is knowing the maximum price you can pay and then having the discipline not to pay a penny more.

The recent bidding war that Bell Atlantic and Vodafone waged to acquire AirTouch Communications illustrates the point that the right price is relative—that is, there's no single correct price for an acquisition. Rumors that Bell Atlantic was in negotiations to acquire AirTouch first surfaced on December 31, 1998. The terms of the Bell Atlantic bid were publicized four days later: it had offered $73 per share, or $45 billion, a 7% premium above AirTouch's closing share price a week earlier of $68. Bell Atlantic's stock price immediately declined by 5%. Clearly, the market did not like the deal.

Vodafone entered the fray on January 7 with a bid of around $55 billion, or $89 per share. Negotiations continued for the next several days until, on January 15, Voda-

Deals with Low Premiums Often Fail—and Vice Versa

As you can see from the 20 deals listed below, the size of the premium does not always correlate with the success of the deal. In half the cases, the acquirers paid a low premium, and their total returns on investment one year later were negative. In the other half, the acquirers paid a high premium, but their total one-year returns were positive. In both cases, we controlled for overall market movements in calculating the returns.

LOW-PREMIUM DEALS WITH LOW RETURNS

	Acquirer's name	Target's name	Premium	One-year market return
1	Marshall & Ilsley	Valley Bancorp	19%	−17%
2	Ceridian	Comdata Holdings	19%	−16%
3	Durco International	BW/IP	14%	−17%
4	3Com	U.S. Robotics	13%	−46%
5	Bergesen	Havtor	11%	−21%
6	AT&T	McCaw Cellular Communications	11%	−17%
7	Dresdner Bank	Kleinwort Benson	10%	−16%
8	Washington Mutual	Great Western Financial	6%	−9%
9	Advanced Micro Devices	NexGen	5%	−59%
10	Ultramar	Diamond Shamrock	1%	−18%

HIGH-PREMIUM DEALS WITH HIGH RETURNS

	Acquirer's name	Target's name	Premium	One-year market return
1	Allegheny Ludlum	Teledyne	115%	33%
2	First Bank System	U.S. Bancorp	85%	12%
3	Northorp	Grumman	65%	12%
4	HealthSouth	Surgical Care Affiliates	61%	30%
5	Praxair	CBI Industries	49%	49%
6	Crompton & Knowles	Uniroyal Chemical	45%	7%
7	Williams Companies	Transco Energy	43%	19%
8	CNA Financial	Continental Corporation	39%	48%
9	Kvaemer	Trafalgar House	35%	15%
10	Frontier	ALC Communications	34%	4%

fone agreed to pay $97 per share, for a total of $62 billion. That price was 33% more than Bell Atlantic's original offer and 43% more than AirTouch's share price before the first rumors of Bell Atlantic's offer had surfaced. Implicit in the deal was the fact that for its shareholders to break even, Vodafone would have to find cost savings and revenue generators worth at least $20 billion. Yet the market liked this deal very much. During the course of this bidding war, Vodafone's stock price actually increased some 14%.

What explains the market's negative reaction to Bell Atlantic's modest premium and its positive reaction to Vodafone's high premium? The answer is that acquiring AirTouch created more valuable synergies for Vodafone than it would have for Bell Atlantic. First of all, Vodafone had a much larger share of the cellular market than Bell Atlantic did in Europe. And as it happened, Vodafone was strong in European countries where AirTouch was not; the two companies complemented each other extremely well. Together, they would create the first complete pan-European cellular telephone company. As a result, they would be able to save a tremendous amount in roaming fees paid to other cellular operators and in interconnection fees paid to fixed line operators. By contrast, a Bell Atlantic–AirTouch combination would not have created a pan-European company, so it had far less potential.

Another source of synergy in the Vodafone-AirTouch deal was the anticipated savings from high-volume purchases of equipment such as handsets, switches, and base stations, which the two companies were already basing on the same technology and buying from the same suppliers. Those savings have been estimated at $330 million, starting in 2002. Finally, having a common European currency will allow Vodafone to use a pan-European flat-rate pricing plan. Should it move in that direction, Vodafone will put tremendous pressure on competitors operating only within each European country. Such rivals would be forced to respond through complicated joint ventures or consolidations. While its competitors engage in these time-consuming and expensive activities, Vodafone would have already digested its acquisition of AirTouch and be one step ahead of the game.

As this example shows, there may be a vast difference between the price one company can pay for an acquisition and the price another can pay. Often the two companies are direct competitors. When they are, the company that can least afford it will be sorely tempted to ignore the financial case and overpay. To do so is nearly always a mistake.

Pricing the Deal

Managers and board members judging the merits of a proposed acquisition need to understand several distinct concepts of value. (See "What's the True Value of an Acquisition?")

INTRINSIC VALUE

The most basic value of the company, its intrinsic value, is based principally on the net present value of expected future cash flows completely independent of any acquisition. That assumes the company continues under current management with whatever revenue growth and performance improvements have already been anticipated by the market. AirTouch's intrinsic value was around $68 per share just before Bell Atlantic's bid.

MARKET VALUE

On top of the intrinsic value, the market may add a premium to reflect the likelihood that an offer for the company will be made (or a higher offer will be tendered than

---

What's the True Value of an Acquisition?

In today's market, the purchase price of an acquisition will nearly always be higher than the intrinsic value of the target company. An acquirer needs to be sure that there are enough cost savings and revenue generators—synergy value—to justify the premium so that the target company's shareholders don't get all the value the deal creates.

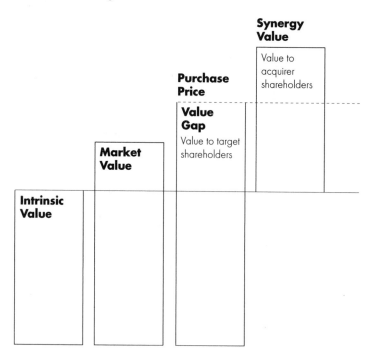

one currently on the table). Market value—commonly called "current market capitalization"—is the same as the share price; it reflects the market participants' valuation of the company. (See "More Deals, More Failures" at the end of this article.) For AirTouch, the market value was $73 per share on December 31, the day the press first reported that a deal with Bell Atlantic was in the works.

PURCHASE PRICE

Wall Street calls this the "anticipated takeout value." It's the price that a bidder anticipates having to pay to be accepted by the target shareholders. For AirTouch, the purchase price turned out to be $97 per share, representing a premium of $29 a share over its intrinsic value.

SYNERGY VALUE

The net present value of the cash flows that will result from improvements made when the companies are combined. These are improvements above and beyond those the market already anticipates each company would make if the acquisition didn't occur, since those are already incorporated into the intrinsic value of each company. Based on the deal price, Vodafone's estimated synergy value was at least $20 billion.

VALUE GAP

The difference between the intrinsic value and the purchase price.

In today's market, both the acquirer and the target company know that the purchase price will be higher than the intrinsic value—in other words, that the buyer will most likely pay a premium.[1] That premium allocates some of the future benefits of the combination to the target shareholders. Absent a premium, most target shareholders would refuse to sell. The acquirer's managers need to figure out just how large a value gap their company can bridge through synergies. The target, meanwhile, will second-guess the acquirer, trying to calculate how high the price can be pushed. If there's more than one potential acquirer and the bidding gets competitive, that places even more upward pressure on the price.

Calculating Synergy Value

There are two keys to success in pricing an acquisition. The first is to make sure that those individuals calculating a target's synergy value are rigorous and that they work with realistic assumptions. The second is to ensure that the acquirer pays no more than it should, no matter how many arm-waving arguments are aired to the effect that "this is a strategic deal; we'd be crazy not to do it!"

Acquirers generally base their calculations on five types of synergies: cost savings, revenue enhancements, process improvements, financial engineering, and tax benefits. The value of each type of synergy will depend on the particular skills and circumstances of the acquirer, something vividly illustrated by the different amounts that Bell Atlantic and Vodafone bid for AirTouch and the market's reaction to those bids.

COST SAVINGS

This is the most common type of synergy and the easiest to estimate. Peter Shaw, head of mergers and acquisitions at the British chemical and pharmaceutical company ICI, refers to cost savings as "hard synergies" and points out that the level of certainty that they will be achieved is quite high. Usually, they come from eliminating jobs, facilities, and related expenses that are no longer needed when functions are consolidated, or they come from economies of scale in purchasing. Cost savings are likely to be especially large when one company acquires another from the same industry in the same country. For example, SBC Communications, the former Southwestern Bell, realized substantial cost savings when it acquired Pacific Telesis. Within the first two years of this merger, SBC saved more than $200 million in information-technology operating and maintenance costs. It also saved tens of millions of dollars by combining the merged companies' purchasing power.

Even though cost savings are the easiest synergy to calculate, overly optimistic projections certainly do occur, so you need to look very carefully at the numbers you're presented with. If you're evaluating projections, be aware of three common problems. First, analysts may overlook the fact that definitions of cost categories vary from company to company. (For example, are warranty costs included in the cost of production or the cost of sales?) So it may appear that there are more easily eliminated costs in a category than turn out to be the case. Second, costs are incurred in different places depending on the structure of each company. Acquirers may assume they can eliminate more corporate or divisional administrative costs than they actually can because essential work is getting done in unexpected places. Third, it is easier to eliminate positions than the people who fill them. Often a job is eliminated on paper, but the person in the job is very talented and must be shifted elsewhere in the company. Therefore, if a consolidation seems to suggest that 200 jobs are destined for the ax, that doesn't mean that 200 salaries are, too.

Acquirers often underestimate how long it will take to realize cost savings. Sometimes that happens because the plans specifying how integration will proceed are insufficiently detailed. In other cases, it happens because the people in both companies are resistant to change, and senior managers often delay making tough cost-cutting decisions. And, of course, the longer it takes for cost savings to be realized, the less value they create.

REVENUE ENHANCEMENTS

It's sometimes possible for an acquirer and its target to achieve a higher level of sales growth together than either company could on its own. Revenue enhancements are notoriously hard to estimate, however, because they involve external variables beyond management's control. The customer base of the acquired company, for instance, may react negatively to different prices and product features. A combined customer base may balk at making too many purchases from a single supplier. And competitors may lower their prices in response to an acquisition. Revenue enhancements are so difficult to predict, in fact, that some wise companies don't even include them when calculating synergy value. Matthew Slatter, the CEO of Bank of Melbourne, says, "We model this [revenue enhancements], but never factor it into the price." Similarly, Peter Shaw at ICI considers them "soft synergies" and discounts them heavily in calculations of synergy value.

Despite their dangers, revenue enhancements can create real value. Sometimes the target brings a superior or complementary product to the more extensive distribution channel of the acquirer. That happened when Lloyds TSB acquired the Cheltenham and Gloucester Building

Society (which had a better home-loan product) and
Abbey Life (which had insurance products). In both
cases, Lloyds TSB was able to sell those products to its
dramatically larger retail customer base, thus generating
more revenue than the three entities could have done
individually. Similarly, having acquired Duracell for a
20% premium, Gillette was confirmed in its expectation
that selling Duracell batteries through Gillette's existing
channels for personal care products would increase sales,
particularly internationally. Gillette sold Duracell products in 25 new markets in the first year after the acquisition and substantially increased sales in established
international markets.

In other instances, a target company's distribution
channel can be used to escalate the sales of the acquiring
company's product. That occurred at Gillette when it
acquired Parker Pen. In calculating what it could pay,
Gillette estimated that it would be able to get an additional $25 million in sales for its own Waterman pens by
taking advantage of Parker's distribution channels.

A final kind of revenue enhancement occurs when the
bigger, postacquisition company gains sufficient critical
mass to attract revenue neither company would have
been able to realize alone. Consider what happened
when ABN and AMRO merged to form ABN AMRO, the
large Dutch bank. Afterward, other large banks pulled
the new company in on syndicated loans that neither
ABN nor AMRO would have been asked to participate in
individually.

PROCESS IMPROVEMENTS

Cost savings result from eliminating duplication or
from purchasing in volume; revenue enhancements are

generated from combining different strengths from the two organizations. Process improvements, by contrast, occur when managers transfer best practices and core competencies from one company to another. That results in both cost savings and revenue enhancements.

The transfer of best practices can flow in either direction. The acquirer may buy a company because the target is especially good at something. Conversely, the acquirer may see that it can drastically improve the target's performance in a key area because of some competence the acquirer has already mastered.

Take the case of National Australia Bank's purchase of Florida mortgage lender HomeSide. HomeSide has an extremely efficient mortgage-servicing process that NAB plans to transfer to its banking operations in Australia, New Zealand, and the United Kingdom. The same was true of ABN AMRO when it acquired the U.S. commercial bank Standard & Federal. In that case, process improvements went hand in hand with cost savings: because its mortgage operation was so efficient, S&F eventually took over the combined bank's entire mortgage business.

Product development processes can also be improved so that new products can be produced at lower cost and get to market faster. Such was the case when Johnson Controls acquired Prince Corporation, a maker of rearview mirrors, door panels, visors, and other parts of automobile interiors. Prince was better than Johnson Controls at understanding customers' needs—both existing and anticipated—and consequently it produced higher-margin products. Prince also had an excellent process for ramping up production of new products, which enabled it to move from design to mass production about twice as fast as Johnson Controls could, maintaining higher quality levels while speeding cycle times.

Johnson learned from Prince and was soon able to apply those advantages to its own products.

For an example of the process improvements an acquiring company can bring to the table, take a look at newspaper giant Gannett. Gannett has a database of financial and nonfinancial measures for each of its 85 newspapers; executives use this rich resource to determine best practices, both boosting revenue and lowering costs. Larry Miller, Gannett's CFO, explains, "We have been able to dramatically improve the papers we've bought. The key for us is knowing in very minute detail how to run a business. This gives us very specific ideas for improvement." Through more efficient production and distribution processes, Gannett has been able to extend its deadlines for news and advertising copy while simultaneously delivering the newspaper more quickly. That helps advertisers and improves Gannett's revenue. Gannett is also able to determine where classified rates are too high, hurting volume, and where they are too low, leaving money on the table. Because it can expect to yield quick, substantial process improvements, Gannett can pay very high premiums for its acquisitions. When you consider that many of the acquisitions are run independently—and so don't offer many consolidation opportunities—the high premiums are quite extraordinary. In fact, Miller has told us, "People are often shocked at what we pay." In nearly all cases, though, performance improvements after the fact have justified the high prices.

The synergies of cost savings, revenue enhancements, and process improvements may be easy to understand conceptually, but our research demonstrates how hard they are to forecast accurately. Why? Most calculations of synergy value occur under horrendous conditions: time pressure is intense, information is limited, and confidentiality must be maintained. Since conditions are so far from ideal, the managers and board members responsible for the final decision should always scrutinize the assumptions underlying the numbers.

FINANCIAL ENGINEERING

Acquirers often think—and hope—that if they borrow cash to finance a transaction, they'll reduce the weighted average cost of capital. That is not a good reason to do a deal. If either the acquirer or the target company could afford to take on more debt, each could have borrowed it on its own.

However, some companies can find genuine synergies through financial engineering. For example, an acquisition can increase the size of a company to a level where there are clear economic benefits to pooling working-capital finance requirements and surplus cash, as well as netting currency positions. These benefits can be quite substantial. When the Credit Suisse Group merged with Winterthur, 10% of the forecasted synergies came from reducing funding costs through optimized capital management.

Here's another genuine financial-engineering synergy: a transaction may allow a company to refinance the target's debt at the acquirer's more favorable borrowing rate without affecting the acquirer's credit rating. That is especially likely to happen in the financial services sector because those companies are big and their risk is diversified.

TAX BENEFITS

Tax considerations are often a barrier that must be overcome to justify a deal, a fact that makes tax-related synergies very difficult to assess. It's useful to distinguish between tax "structuring," which makes the deal possible, and tax "engineering" (also called tax planning), which ensures that the overall tax rate of the combined company is equal to or lower than the blended tax rates of the two companies before the deal. Regulators often believe that companies using perfectly legitimate structuring and engineering techniques to avoid incurring additional costs are simply taking advantage of loopholes. Thus companies are not anxious to disclose any clever techniques they may have used.

The goal of tax structuring is to avoid as many one-time tax costs as possible. Those costs may include capital and transfer duties, as well as change-of-ownership provisions that can trigger capital gains or prevent tax losses from being carried forward.

Assuming that analysts have identified structuring techniques that make the deal feasible, it is then possible to look for real tax-related synergies. One of the most common is the transfer of brands and other intellectual property to a low-tax subsidiary. But there are a host of other potential synergies: placing shared services and central purchasing in tax-advantaged locations; reorganizing within a country to pool taxes; pushing down debt into high-tax subsidiaries; and obtaining tax benefits that neither company could have realized on its own.

Assume that the numbers don't add up, but people in the company still claim there are compelling strategic reasons for doing the deal anyway. What next? The most disciplined thing to do is walk away.

Even when real benefits can be obtained from tax engineering, companies should not make deals based on those benefits alone. The reason to pursue a merger or an acquisition is to achieve a better competitive position in the marketplace—a lower cost structure, for example, or a better platform for growth. While financial and tax-engineering tactics can produce value for shareholders, by themselves they do not strengthen a company's competitive position.

"We have a rule on the Executive Committee," says Harry Tempest of ABN AMRO. "When someone says 'strategic,' the rest of us say, 'too expensive.'"

Furthermore, the difficulty of integrating two companies can overwhelm purely financial and tax benefits.

On Doing Deals for Strategic Reasons

Assume that synergy value has been calculated extremely carefully and the numbers don't add up, but people in the company still claim there are compelling strategic reasons for doing the deal anyway. What next?

The most disciplined thing to do is walk away. If the numbers don't work, it's not a good deal. That's the practice at ABN AMRO, says Harry Tempest. "We have a rule on the Executive Committee. When someone says 'strategic,' the rest of us say, 'too expensive.'"

Doubtless there are deals that should happen for strategic reasons even when the numbers don't sound promising, but they are few and far between. Before undertaking such an acquisition, senior managers should look with extraordinary rigor at the emotional state of those backing the deal—and then at the strategic reasons themselves.

First, the emotional atmosphere. A lot of deals happen because managers fall in love with the idea of the deal. Successful executives, after all, are competitive people who hate to lose, and nothing brings out the competitive juices like going after another company, particularly when one's rivals are in hot pursuit. Anyone who has lived through a deal can tell you how exciting it can get. But as Tempest says, "You have to be careful not to let the thrill of the chase get the testosterone flowing."

Two of the most common arguments for ignoring the numbers are especially dangerous. When you hear someone say, "It's the last deal of its kind," beware. It's never the last deal. Deals fall apart all the time—and what's more, divestitures are nearly as common as acquisitions in today's market. Assets unavailable today could easily be up for sale tomorrow.

The second argument is, "If you don't acquire a target, a major competitor will." But the fact is, if the numbers don't work for you, you should let your rival have the target company. Often that company will overpay and weaken its own competitive position. Better it than you.

If you feel compelled to move forward with a deal when the numbers tell you to stop, analyze the strategic reasons themselves as rigorously as you can. Remember that most strategic reasons to do deals boil down to some form of revenue generator or cost savings, which should be reflected in the numbers. Poke holes in the arguments and see if they still hold up. What could go wrong? What if the assumptions about the direction of technology and prices are wrong? What regulatory changes could make the deal fail, and how likely are they to occur? How could competitors react to the deal in ways that could hurt you—even if

Doubtless there are deals that should happen for strategic reasons even when the numbers don't sound promising, but they are few and far between.

they hurt themselves as well? Make sure that the group reviewing acquisition candidates includes strong skeptics with persuasive voices.

It may also make sense to introduce more sophisticated analytical techniques. Real-options valuation, for example, can help managers quantify potential, but not definite, future benefits. (See Timothy A. Luehrman's "Investment Opportunities as Real Options: Getting Started on the Numbers," HBR July–August 1998.) That approach calculates a value for each of the options that the deal creates. Thus if the target company is developing a new, potentially valuable technology that could change the rules of competition in your industry, analysts can use real-options techniques to quantify the value of that technology based on a range of possible outcomes. For example, value can be realized by licensing the technology to others, by selling it off, or by investing in it further to develop a commercial product. Real-options thinking can also help managers identify the decisions they will have to make about future investments or other courses of action, and when those decisions need to be made.

Organizational Discipline and Pricing

Successful acquiring companies know how to calculate synergy value, and they know how to walk away from a deal that seems fabulous until someone runs the numbers. (See "Weak Links" at the end of this article.) However, they also know that sometimes human nature takes over in the heat of an exciting deal, and so they have developed process disciplines that help them stick to what the numbers tell them.

Many companies don't allow the negotiating manager to price the deal for fear that he or she will become too personally invested and overpay. Often a higher-level manager sets a price ceiling before negotiations begin; any negotiator or business-unit manager who wants to go over the ceiling must explain why and get explicit approval. Hutchison Whampoa and AlliedSignal both use that approach. In fact, AlliedSignal's CEO, Larry Bossidy, has ultimate authority over all prices unless a deal is so large that it requires board approval.

The Interpublic Group of Companies (IPG) has a different approach to discipline. The large advertising and marketing-communications company has made more than 400 acquisitions in the past 15 years; because the group has been so active, a lot of the pricing and negotiations have to occur at the business-unit level. The company has decreed that every target has to achieve at least a 12% return on investment within five to seven years. In addition, operating managers are required to meet operating targets within five years. And those requirements are backed up with messages that managers understand. Says Gene Beard, vice chairman of finance and operations, "Failure to meet these targets significantly lowers the long-term incentive awards our managers receive."

Frank Borelli, the CFO of Marsh & McLennan, has a good example of how strict process discipline can pay off. Within Marsh & McLennan, which offers insurance services, investment management, and human-resource-management consulting, Borelli is adamant about three criteria for doing any deal. The deal has to earn at least the company's cost of capital, it can't dilute earnings, and the target company's growth rate has to be higher than Marsh & McLennan's itself.

In the 1990s, the company had the chance to acquire two companies in the consolidating insurance-brokerage industry: Frank B. Hall in 1992 and Alexander & Alexander in 1996. The top managers in the insurance services unit were anxious to pursue both deals. However, neither company met all three criteria, and Borelli refused to bend the rules. The insurance services executives were dismayed when a major competitor, Aon, acquired both companies. When an opportunity to buy Minet came along in late 1996, the insurance services executives were more anxious than ever to do the deal. However, Borelli resisted that one as well. He thought it could be what he termed a "huge disaster" because Marsh & McLennan could not protect itself against contingent liabilities. By that point, the insurance services executives "were really upset with me, to say the least," Borelli says.

In March of 1997, a fourth opportunity presented itself: this time, the target was a top-rate competitor, Johnson & Higgins. That acquisition met Borelli's three criteria and created substantial value for the company. By resisting the temptation to do unattractive deals even when a major competitor was also considering them, Marsh & McLennan left itself in a good position to take advantage of a better opportunity when it came along. Borelli believes that if Marsh & McLennan had acquired the much less attractive Alexander & Alexander, it would not have been in a position to acquire Johnson & Higgins. "You can only digest so much," he says.

Another example of discipline in the pricing process comes from Saint-Gobain, the French manufacturing and distribution company. Every acquisition is expected to improve its prior year's return on equity in the first year after being acquired and exceed its preacquisition return on assets by the third year. CFO Jean-François Phelizon explains that Saint-Gobain takes a global approach to analyzing its acquisitions: "We compare the value created by the acquisition to the value that could be created by buying back our own shares." If the latter generates more value, the acquisition is not made.

Some companies routinely review each completed acquisition rigorously to better understand what makes for success or failure. That, too, is a form of process discipline. Other companies keep data on the performance of previous acquisitions to help them price future deals. Nearly all the companies in our study used some kind of a posttransaction-monitoring process to track how well the acquisition or merger was performing relative to expectations and to draw lessons about what should be done differently in the future.

The lessons on pricing acquisitions and mergers that we've outlined here are straightforward. In fact, they may strike readers as simple common sense. We would not disagree with that judgment. Yet the fact remains that over half the deals being done today will destroy value for the acquiring company's shareholders.

What's the reason for the disparity between these simple lessons and these poor results? We believe that far too many companies neglect the organizational discipline needed to ensure that analytical rigor triumphs over emotion and ego. Such discipline is the responsibility of executive managers and the board of directors. If the returns to shareholders from acquisitions and mergers over the next ten years are no better than they have been for the past 100, it will be because companies have not created systematic corporate governance processes that put these simple lessons into practice.

More Deals, More Failures

PRICING AN ACQUISITION CORRECTLY is extraordinarily important given how many deals there are—and how many fail. During the past decade, merger and acquisition activity has steadily increased, as measured both by the total number of deals and by the value of those deals. In 1998 alone, 20,448 deals were completed worth a total of $2 trillion.

The prognosis for most of those deals is not good. Several studies covering M&A activity in the past 75 years have concluded that well over half of mergers and acquisitions failed to create their expected value. In many cases, value was destroyed, and the company's performance after the deal was significantly below what it had been before the deal. The success rate is not much better today than it was 75 years ago, despite numerous, well-publicized studies illuminating the high failure rates.[2]

The executives who continue to make bad deals don't appear to have learned much. The equity markets, by contrast, *have* learned from experience. Building on research done by Mark Sirower, we studied 131 deals, each valued at $500 million or more, that took place between 1994 and 1997 in the United States, Europe, and Asia. Our analysis, consistent with Sirower's earlier study of U.S. companies, shows that in 59% of the deals, the total market-adjusted return of the acquiring company went down on announcement.[3] That means the market thought the deal would destroy rather than create value for the shareholders of the acquiring or merged company. Returns for 71% of those deals were negative over the next 12 months. By contrast, of the 41% of deals where the total return went up on announcement—in other words, where the market expected value to be created—55% still had positive returns in the ensuing year. This analysis demonstrates both that most deals do not create value and that the market is fairly good at predicting which ones will and which ones won't.

Weak Links

OUR RESEARCH FOCUSED ON highly competent acquirers. Nevertheless, we have identified two areas that even these successful companies felt could be improved.

The first is risk analysis. Although, in the course of determining their bid price, all the companies we studied performed detailed financial and operating analyses, including sensitivity analysis, few of them did a rigorous risk analysis that examined what the least and most favorable outcomes could be. The downside analysis was particularly weak, given the built-in bias toward optimistic assumptions to make the numbers justify the deal.

When analyzing the downside, managers should ask themselves, "What could cause this deal to fail?" Depending on the industry and the country, that could be a dramatic and unanticipated new technology, a new nationalistic political regime, or new regulations resulting from a successful lawsuit. We suspect that in the future more companies will pay attention to this crucial task, particularly for very large deals. The analysis may well suggest that even when the probability of a disaster is low, if the consequences are very significant, the deal should not be done. As Bob Prowse, the finance director of National Australia Bank, says, "The price of making a mistake is greater than the price of missing an opportunity."

The second area where even the best companies can improve their practices is in external communication to the capital markets, customers, suppliers, regulatory bodies, and geographic communities. Companies that have substantial M&A experience generally do a good job of communicating with employees, both before and after the deal closes. However, it is equally important to explain to external stakeholders what the benefits of the deal are and how the stakeholders will be affected, both positively and negatively.

The reason it's important that the capital markets understand the deal is obvious; their short-term reaction can make managers' lives miserable—or delightful. Bob Bauman, who became CEO of SmithKline Beecham after it was formed from the merger of SmithKline Beckman and Beecham Group, felt that communication to the market was one weak spot in an otherwise very successful merger. "The marketplace has to have measures—and lots of them. We gave them a lot of clarity about the end results we were aiming for, but insufficient detail on the milestones along the way. We could have done a better job here."

Bauman's comment reflects the importance of quantifying the value of expected synergies and reporting the progress made in achieving them. When that's done well, a company's credibility grows, which, in turn, is reflected in the stock price. Failure to communicate credibly will have the opposite effect.

Notes

1. The usual exceptions are when someone negotiates to buy a privately held company or in a stock-for-stock merger transaction when the two companies are of comparable size and value. However, premiums can even be paid in stock deals, especially when one company is much smaller than the other or when a disproportionate amount of the synergies will be obtained from one of the companies.

2. For a good summary of these studies, see Dennis C. Mueller, "Mergers: Theory and Evidence," in *Mergers, Markets and Public Policy,* ed. G. Mussati (Kluwer Academic Publishers, 1995).

3. Mark Sirower, *The Synergy Trap* (The Free Press, 1997).

Originally published in July–August 1999
Reprint 99402

Stock or Cash?

The Trade-Offs for Buyers and Sellers in Mergers and Acquisitions

ALFRED RAPPAPORT AND
MARK L. SIROWER

Executive Summary

IN 1988, LESS THEN 2% OF large deals were paid for entirely in stock; by 1998, that number had risen to 50%. The shift has profound ramifications for shareholders of both the acquiring and acquired companies. In this article, the authors provide a framework and two simple tools to guide boards of both companies through the issues they need to consider when making decisions about how to pay for—and whether to accept—a deal.

First an acquirer has to decide whether to finance the deal using stock or pay cash. Second, if the acquirer decides to issue stock, it then must decide whether to offer a fixed value of shares or a fixed number of them. Offering cash places all the potential risks and rewards with the acquirer—and sends a strong signal to the markets that it has confidence in the value not only of the deal but in its own stock. By issuing shares, however, an acquirer in essence offers to share the newly merged company with the stockholders of the acquired company—a signal the market often interprets as a lack of confidence in the value of the acquirer's stock. Offering a fixed number of shares reinforces that impression because it requires the selling stockholders to share the risk that the value of the acquirer's stock will decline before the deal goes through. Offering a fixed value of shares sends a more confident signal to the markets, as the acquirer assumes all of that risk.

The choice between cash and stock should never be made without full and careful consideration of the potential consequences. The all-too-frequent disappointing returns from stock transactions underscore how important the method of payment truly is.

THE LEGENDARY MERGER MANIA of the 1980s pales beside the M&A activity of this decade. In 1998 alone, 12,356 deals involving U.S. targets were announced for a total value of $1.63 trillion. Compare that with the 4,066 deals worth $378.9 billion announced in 1988, at the height of the 1980s merger movement. But the numbers should be no surprise. After all, acquisitions remain the quickest route companies have to new markets and to new capabilities. As markets globalize, and the pace at which technologies change continues to accelerate, more and more companies are finding mergers and acquisitions to be a compelling strategy for growth.

What is striking about acquisitions in the 1990s, however, is the way they're being paid for. In 1988, nearly 60% of the value of large deals—those over $100 million—was paid for entirely in cash. Less than 2% was paid for in stock. But just ten years later, the profile is almost reversed: 50% of the value of all large deals in 1998 was paid for entirely in stock, and only 17% was paid for entirely in cash.

This shift has profound ramifications for the shareholders of both acquiring and acquired companies. In a cash deal, the roles of the two parties are clear-cut, and the exchange of money for shares completes a simple transfer of ownership. But in an exchange of shares, it becomes far less clear who is the buyer and who is the seller.

In a cash deal, the roles of the two parties are clear-cut, but in a stock deal, it's less clear who is the buyer and who is the seller.

In some cases, the shareholders of the acquired company can end up owning most of the company that bought their shares. Companies that pay for their acquisitions with stock share both the value and the risks of the transaction with the shareholders of the company they acquire. The decision to use stock instead of cash can also affect shareholder returns. In studies covering more than 1,200 major deals, researchers have consistently found that, at the time of announcement, shareholders of acquiring companies fare worse in stock transactions than they do in cash transactions. What's more, the findings show that early performance differences between cash and stock transactions become greater—much greater—over time.

Despite their obvious importance, these issues are often given short shrift in corporate boardrooms and the pages of the financial press. Both managers and journalists tend to focus mostly on the prices paid for acquisitions. It's not that focusing on price is wrong. Price is certainly an important issue confronting both sets of shareholders. But when companies are considering making—or accepting—an offer for an exchange of shares, the valuation of the company in play becomes just one of several factors that managers and investors need to consider. In this article, we provide a framework to guide the boards of both the acquiring and the selling companies through their decision-making process, and we offer two simple tools to help managers quantify the risks involved to their shareholders in offering or accepting stock. But first let's look at the basic differences between stock deals and cash deals.

Cash Versus Stock Trade-Offs

The main distinction between cash and stock transactions is this: In cash transactions, acquiring shareholders take on the entire risk that the expected synergy value embedded in the acquisition premium will not materialize. In stock transactions, that risk is shared with selling shareholders. More precisely, in stock transactions, the synergy risk is shared in proportion to the percentage of the combined company the acquiring and selling shareholders each will own.

To see how that works, let's look at a hypothetical example. Suppose that Buyer Inc. wants to acquire its competitor, Seller Inc. The market capitalization of Buyer Inc. is $5 billion, made up of 50 million shares priced at $100 per share. Seller Inc.'s market capitalization stands at $2.8 billion—40 million shares each worth $70. The managers of Buyer Inc. estimate that by merging the two companies, they can create an additional synergy value of $1.7 billion. They announce an offer to buy all the shares of Seller Inc. at $100 per share. The value placed on Seller Inc. is therefore $4 billion, representing a premium of $1.2 billion over the company's preannouncement market value of $2.8 billion.

The expected net gain to the acquirer from an acquisition—we call it the *shareholder value added* (SVA)—is the difference between the estimated value of the synergies obtained through the acquisition and the acquisition premium. So if Buyer Inc. chooses to pay cash for the deal, then the SVA for its shareholders is simply the expected synergy of $1.7 billion minus the $1.2 billion premium, or $500 million.

But if Buyer Inc. decides to finance the acquisition by issuing new shares, the SVA for its existing stockholders will drop. Let's suppose that Buyer Inc. offers one of its shares for each of Seller Inc.'s shares. The new offer places the same value on Seller Inc. as did the cash offer. But upon the deal's completion, the acquiring shareholders will find that their ownership in Buyer Inc. has been reduced. They will own only 55.5% of a new total of 90 million shares outstanding after the acquisition. So their share of the acquisition's expected SVA is only 55.5% of $500 million, or $277.5 million. The rest goes to Seller Inc.'s shareholders, who are now shareholders in an enlarged Buyer Inc.

The only way that Buyer Inc.'s original shareholders can obtain the same SVA from a stock deal as from a cash deal would be by offering Seller Inc. fewer new shares, justifying this by pointing out that each share would be worth more if the expected synergies were included. In other words, the new shares would reflect the value that Buyer Inc.'s managers believe the combined company will be worth rather than the $100-per-share preannouncement market value. But while that kind of deal sounds fair in principle, in practice Seller Inc.'s stockholders would be unlikely to accept fewer shares unless they were convinced that the valuation of the merged company will turn out to be even greater than Buyer Inc.'s managers estimate. In light of the disappointing track record of acquirers, this is a difficult sell at best.

On the face of it, then, stock deals offer the acquired company's shareholders the chance to profit from the potential synergy gains that the acquiring shareholders expect to make above and beyond the premium. That's certainly what the acquirers will tell them. The problem, of course, is that the stockholders of the acquired company also have to share the risks. Let's suppose that Buyer Inc. completes the purchase of Seller Inc. with an exchange of shares and then none of the expected synergies materialize. In an all-cash deal, Buyer Inc.'s shareholders would shoulder the entire loss of the $1.2 billion premium paid for Seller Inc. But in a share deal, their loss is only 55.5% of the premium. The remaining 44.5% of the loss—$534 million—is borne by Seller Inc.'s shareholders.

In many takeover situations, of course, the acquirer will be so much larger than the target that the selling shareholders will end up owning only a negligible proportion of the combined company. But as the evidence suggests, stock financing is proving particularly popular in large deals (see "The Popularity of Paper"). In those cases, the potential risks for the acquired shareholders are large, as ITT's stockholders found out after their company was taken over by Starwood Lodging. It is one of the highest profile takeover stories of the 1990s, and it vividly illustrates the perils of being paid in paper.

The story started in January 1997 with an offer by Hilton Hotels of $55 per share for ITT, a 28% premium over ITT's preoffer share price. Under the terms of the offer, ITT's shareholders would receive $27.50 in cash

The Popularity of Paper

These graphs illustrate the degree to which companies have paid for their acquisitions with paper. They also show that stock is particularly popular for larger transactions because the value of stock deals has grown faster than the number of stock deals.

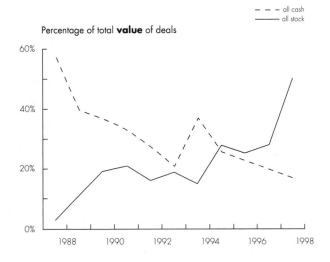

Percentage of total **value** of deals

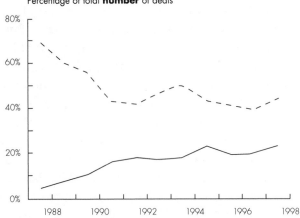

Percentage of total **number** of deals

Source: Securities Data Company

and the balance in Hilton stock. In the face of stiff resistance from ITT, Hilton raised its bid in August to $70 per share. At that point, a new bidder, Starwood Lodging, a real estate investment trust with extensive hotel holdings, entered the fray with a bid of $82 per share. Starwood proposed paying $15 in cash and $67 in its own shares.

In response, Hilton announced a bid of $80 per share in this form—ITT shareholders would receive $80 per share in cash for 55% of their shares and two shares of Hilton stock for each of the remaining 45% of their shares. If the stock did not reach at least $40 per share one year after the merger, Hilton would make up the shortfall to a maximum of $12 per share. In essence, then, Hilton was offering the equivalent of an all-cash bid that would be worth at least $80 per share if Hilton's shares traded at $28 or higher one year after the merger. Hilton's management believed it would clinch the deal with this lower bid by offering more cash and protecting the future value of its shares.

Starwood countered by raising its offer to $85 per share. This time, it gave ITT's shareholders the option to take payment entirely in stock or entirely in cash. But there was a catch: if more than 60% of the stockholders chose the cash option, then the cash payout to those shareholders would be capped at just $25.50, and the balance would be paid in Starwood stock. Despite this catch, ITT's board voted to recommend the Starwood offer over the less risky Hilton offer, and it was then approved by shareholders. Ironically, while ITT's board chose the offer with the larger stock component, the stockholders actually had a strong preference for cash. When the votes were counted, almost 75% of ITT's shareholders had selected Starwood's cash option—a percentage far greater than publicly predicted by Starwood's management and which, of course, triggered the $25.50 cap.

As a consequence of accepting Starwood's offer, ITT's shareholders ended up owning 67% of the combined company's shares. That was because even before the bid was announced (with its very substantial premium), ITT's market value was almost twice as large as Starwood's. ITT's shareholders were left very exposed, and they suffered for it. Although Starwood's share price held steady at around $55 during the takeover, the price plunged after completion. A year later, it stood at $32 per share. At that price, the value of Starwood's offer had shrunk from $85 to $64 for those ITT shareholders who had elected cash. Shareholders who had chosen to be paid entirely in stock fared even worse: their package of Starwood shares was worth only $49. ITT's shareholders had paid a steep price for choosing the nominally higher but riskier Starwood offer.

Fixed Shares or Fixed Value?

Boards and shareholders must do more than simply choose between cash and stock when making—or accepting—an offer. There are two ways to structure an offer for an exchange of shares, and the choice of one approach or the other has a significant impact on the allocation of risk between the two sets of shareholders. Companies can either issue a fixed number of shares or they can issue a fixed value of shares.

FIXED SHARES

In these offers, the number of shares to be issued is certain, but the value of the deal may fluctuate between the announcement of the offer and the closing date, depending on the acquirer's share price. Both acquiring and selling shareholders are affected by those changes, but changes in the acquirer's price will not affect the proportional ownership of the two sets of shareholders in the combined company. Therefore, the interests of the two sets of shareholders in the deal's shareholder value added do not change, even though the actual SVA may turn out to be different than expected.

In a fixed-share deal, shareholders in the acquired company are particularly vulnerable to a fall in the price of the acquiring company's stock because they have to bear a portion of the price risk from the time the deal is announced. That was precisely what happened to shareholders of Green Tree Financial when in 1998 it accepted a $7.2 billion offer by the insurance company Conseco. Under the terms of the deal, each of Green Tree's common shares was converted into 0.9165 of a share of Conseco common stock. On April 6, a day before the deal was announced, Conseco was trading at $57.75 per share. At that price, Green Tree's shareholders would receive just under $53 worth of Conseco stock for each of their Green Tree shares. That represented a huge 83% premium over Green Tree's preannouncement share price of $29.

Conseco's rationale for the deal was that it needed to serve more of the needs of middle-income consumers. The vision articulated when the deal was announced was that Conseco would sell its insurance and annuity products along with Green Tree's consumer loans, thereby strengthening both businesses. But the acquisition was not without its risks. First, the Green Tree deal was more than eight times larger than the largest deal Conseco had ever completed and almost 20 times the average size of its past 20 deals. Second, Green Tree was in the business of lending money to buyers of mobile homes, a business very different from Conseco's, and the deal would require a costly postmerger integration effort.

The market was skeptical of the cross-selling synergies and of Conseco's ability to compete in a new business. Conseco's growth had been built on a series of highly successful acquisitions in its core businesses of life and health insurance, and the market took Conseco's diversification as a signal that acquisition opportunities in those businesses were getting scarce. So investors started to sell Conseco shares. By the time the deal closed at the end of June 1998, Conseco's share price had fallen from $57.75 to $48. That fall immediately hit Green Tree's shareholders as well as Conseco's. Instead of the expected $53, Green Tree's shareholders received $44 for each of their shares—the premium had fallen from 83% to 52%.

Green Tree's shareholders who held on to their Conseco stock after closing lost even more. By April 1999, one year after announcement, Conseco's share price had fallen to $30. At that price, Green Tree's shareholders lost not only the entire premium but also an additional $1.50 per share from the preannouncement value.

FIXED VALUE

The other way to structure a stock deal is for the acquirer to issue a fixed value of shares. In these deals, the number of shares issued is not fixed until the closing date and depends on the prevailing price. As a result, the proportional ownership of the ongoing company is left in doubt until closing. To see how fixed-value deals work, let's go back to Buyer Inc. and Seller Inc. Suppose that Buyer Inc.'s offer is to be paid in stock but that at the closing date its share price has fallen by exactly the premium it is paying for Seller Inc.—from $100 per share to $76 per share. At that share price, in a fixed-value deal, Buyer Inc. has to issue 52.6 million shares to give Seller Inc.'s shareholders their promised $4 billion worth. But that leaves Buyer Inc.'s original shareholders with just 48.7% of the combined company instead of the 55.5% they would have had in a fixed-share deal.

As the illustration suggests, in a fixed-value deal, the acquiring company bears all the price risk on its shares between announcement and closing. If the stock price falls, the acquirer must issue additional shares to pay sellers their contracted fixed-dollar value. So the acquiring company's shareholders have to accept a lower stake in the combined company, and their share of the expected SVA falls correspondingly. Yet in our experience, companies rarely incorporate this potentially significant risk into their SVA calculations despite the fact that the acquirer's stock price decreases in a substantial majority of cases. (See "How Risk Is Distributed Between Acquirer and Seller.")

By the same token, the owners of the acquired company are better protected in a fixed-value deal. They are not exposed to any loss in value until after the deal has closed. In our example, Seller Inc.'s shareholders will not have to bear any synergy risk at all because the shares they receive now incorporate no synergy expectations in their price. The loss in the share price is made up by granting the selling shareholders extra shares. And if, after closing, the market reassesses the acquisition and Buyer Inc.'s stock price does rise, Seller Inc.'s shareholders will enjoy higher returns because of the increased percentage they own in the combined company. However, if Buyer Inc.'s stock price continues to deteriorate after the closing date, Seller Inc.'s shareholders will bear a greater percentage of those losses.

How Risk Is Distributed Between Acquirer and Seller

The way an acquisition is paid for determines how the risk is distributed between the buyer and the seller. An acquirer that pays entirely in cash, for example, assumes all the risk that the price of its shares will drop between the announcement of the deal and its closing. The acquirer also assumes all the operating risk after the deal closes. By contrast, an acquirer that pays the seller a fixed number of its own shares limits its risk from a drop in share price to the percentage it will own of the new, merged company. The acquirer that pays a fixed value of shares assumes the entire preclosing market risk but limits its operating risk to the percentage of its postclosing ownership in the new company.

	Preclosing market risk	Postclosing operating risk
All-Cash Deal		
Acquirer	all	all
Seller	none	none
Fixed-Share Deal		
Acquirer	expected percentage of ownership	actual percentage of ownership
Seller	expected percentage of ownernship	actual percentage of ownership
Fixed-Value Deal		
Acquirer	all	actual percentage of ownership
Seller	none	actual percentage of ownership

How Can Companies Choose?

Given the dramatic effects on value that the method of payment can have, boards of both acquiring and selling companies have a fiduciary responsibility to incorporate those effects into their decision-making processes.

If the acquirer believes the market is undervaluing its shares, it should not issue new shares to finance an acquisition.

Acquiring companies must be able to explain to their stockholders why they have to share the synergy gains of the transaction with the stockholders of the acquired company. For their part, the acquired company's shareholders, who are being offered stock in the combined company, must be made to understand the risks of what is, in reality, a new investment. All this makes the job of the board members more complex. We'll look first at the issues faced by the board of an acquiring company.

QUESTIONS FOR THE ACQUIRER

The management and the board of an acquiring company should address three economic questions before deciding on a method of payment. First, are the acquiring company's shares undervalued, fairly valued, or overvalued? Second, what is the risk that the expected synergies needed to pay for the acquisition premium will not materialize? The answers to these questions will help guide companies in making the decision between a cash and a stock offer. Finally, how likely is it that the value of the acquiring company's shares will drop before closing? (See "Why the Market Is Skeptical About Acquisitions" at the end of this article.) The answer to that question should guide the decision between a fixed-value and a fixed-share offer. Let's look at each question in turn:

Valuation of acquirer's shares. If the acquirer believes that the market is undervaluing its shares, then it should not issue new shares to finance a transaction because to do so would penalize current shareholders. Research consistently shows that the market takes the issuance of stock by a company as a sign that the company's managers—who are in a better position to know about its long-term prospects—believe the stock to be overvalued. Thus, when management chooses to use stock to finance an acquisition, there's plenty of reason to expect that company's stock to fall.

What's more, companies that use stock to pay for an acquisition often base the price of the new shares on the current, undervalued market price rather than on the higher value they believe their shares to be worth. That can cause a company to pay more than it intends and in some cases to pay more than the acquisition is *A really confident acquirer* worth. Suppose that our *would be expected to pay for* hypothetical acquirer, *the acquisition with cash.* Buyer Inc., believed that its shares are worth $125 rather than $100. Its managers should value the 40 million shares it plans to issue to Seller Inc.'s shareholders at $5 billion, not $4 billion. Then if Buyer Inc. thinks Seller Inc. is worth only $4 billion, it ought to offer the shareholders no more than 32 million shares.

Of course, in the real world, it's not easy to convince a disbelieving seller to accept fewer but "more valuable" shares—as we have already pointed out. So if an acquiring company's managers believe that the market significantly undervalues their shares, their logical course is to proceed with a cash offer. Yet we consistently find that the same CEOs who publicly declare their company's share price to be too low will cheerfully issue large amounts of stock at that "too low" price to pay for their acquisitions. Which signal is the market more likely to follow?

Synergy risks. The decision to use stock or cash also sends signals about the acquirer's estimation of the risks of failing to achieve the expected synergies from the deal. A really confident acquirer would be expected to pay for the acquisition with cash so that its shareholders would not have to give any of the anticipated merger gains to the acquired company's shareholders. But if managers believe the risk of not achieving the required level of synergy is substantial, they can be expected to try to hedge their bets by offering stock. By diluting their company's ownership interest, they will also limit participation in any losses incurred either before or after the deal goes through. Once again, though, the market is well able to draw its own conclusions. Indeed, empirical research consistently finds that the market reacts significantly more favorably to announcements of cash deals than to announcements of stock deals.

Stock offers, then, send two powerful signals to the market: that the acquirer's shares are overvalued and that its management lacks confidence in the acquisition. In principle, therefore, a company that is confident about integrating an acquisition successfully, and that believes its own shares to be undervalued, should always proceed with a cash offer. A cash offer neatly resolves the valuation problem for acquirers that believe they are undervalued as well as for sellers uncertain of the acquiring company's true value. But it's not always so straightforward. Quite often, for example, a company does not have sufficient cash resources—or debt capacity—to make a cash offer. In that case, the decision is much less clearcut, and the board must judge whether the additional costs associated with issuing undervalued shares still justify the acquisition.

Preclosing market risk. A board that has determined to proceed with a share offer still has to decide how to structure it. That decision depends on an assessment of the risk that the price of the acquiring company's shares will drop between the announcement of the deal and its closing.

Research has shown that the market responds more favorably when acquirers demonstrate their confidence in the value of their own shares through their willingness to bear more preclosing market risk. In a 1997 article in the *Journal of Finance,* for example, Joel Houston and Michael Ryngaert found in a large sample of banking mergers that the more sensitive the seller's compensation is to changes in the acquirer's stock price, the less favorable is the market's response to the acquisition announcement. That leads to the logical guideline that the greater the potential impact of preclosing market risk, the more important it is for the acquirer to signal its confidence by assuming some of that risk.

A fixed-share offer is not a confident signal since the seller's compensation drops if the value of the acquirer's shares falls. Therefore, the fixed-share approach should be adopted only if the preclosing market risk is relatively low. That's more likely (although not necessarily) the case when the acquiring and selling companies are in the same or closely related industries. Common economic forces govern the share prices of both companies, and thus the negotiated exchange ratio is more likely to remain equitable to acquirers and sellers at closing.

But there are ways for an acquiring company to structure a fixed-share offer without sending signals to the market that its stock is overvalued. The acquirer, for example, can protect the seller against a fall in the acquirer's share price below a specified floor level by guaranteeing a minimum price. (Acquirers that offer such a floor typically also insist on a ceiling on the total value of shares distributed to sellers.) Establishing a floor not only reduces preclosing market risk for sellers but also diminishes the probability that the seller's board will back out of the deal or that its shareholders will not approve the transaction. That might have helped Bell Atlantic in its bid for TCI in 1994—which would have been the largest deal in history at the time. Bell Atlantic's stock fell sharply in the weeks following the announcement, and the deal—which included no market-risk protection—unraveled as a result.

An even more confident signal is given by a fixed-value offer in which sellers are assured of a stipulated market value while acquirers bear the entire cost of any decline in their share price before closing. If the market believes in the merits of the offer, then the acquirer's price may even rise, enabling it to issue fewer shares to the seller's stockholders. The acquirer's shareholders, in that event, would retain a greater proportion of the deal's SVA. As with fixed-share offers, floors and ceilings can be attached to fixed-value offers—in the form of the number of shares to be issued. A ceiling ensures that the interests of the acquirer's shareholders are not severely diluted if the share price falls before the deal closes. A floor guarantees the selling shareholders a minimum number of shares and a minimum level of participation in the expected SVA should the acquirer's stock price rise appreciably.

QUESTIONS FOR THE SELLER

In the case of a cash offer, the selling company's board faces a fairly straightforward task. It just has to compare the value of the company as an independent business against the price offered. The only risks are that it could hold out for a higher price or that management could create better value if the company remained independent. The latter case certainly can be hard to justify. Let's suppose that the shareholders of our hypothetical acquisition, Seller Inc., are offered $100 per share, representing a 43% premium over the current $70 price. Let's also suppose that they can get a 10% return by putting that cash in investments with a similar level of risk. After five years, the $100 would compound to $161. If the bid were rejected, Seller Inc. would have to earn an annual return of 18% on its currently valued $70 shares to do as well. So uncertain a return must compete against a bird in the hand.

More than likely, though, the selling company's board will be offered stock or some combination of cash and stock and so will also have to value the shares of the combined company being offered to its shareholders. In essence, shareholders of the acquired company will be partners in the postmerger enterprise and will therefore have as much interest in realizing the synergies as the shareholders of the acquiring company. If the expected synergies do not materialize or if other disappointing information develops after closing, selling shareholders may well lose a significant portion of the premium received on their shares. So if a selling company's board accepts an exchange-of-shares offer, it is not only endorsing the offer as a fair price for its own shares, it is also endorsing the idea that the combined company is an attractive investment. Essentially, then, the board must act in the role of a buyer as well as a seller and must go through the same decision process that the acquiring company follows.

At the end of the day, however, no matter how a stock offer is made, selling shareholders should never assume that the announced value is the value they will realize before or after closing. Selling early may limit exposure, but that strategy carries costs because the shares of target companies almost invariably trade below the offer price during the preclosing period. Of course, shareholders who wait until after the closing date to sell their shares of the merged company have no way of knowing what those shares will be worth at that time.

The questions we have discussed here—How much is the acquirer worth? How likely is it that the expected synergies will be realized?, and How great is the preclosing market risk?—address the economic issues associated with the decisions to offer or accept a particular method of paying for a merger or acquisition. There are other, less important, issues of tax treatment and accounting that the advisers of both boards will seek to bring to their attention (see "Tax Consequences of Acquisitions" and "Accounting: Seeing Through the Smoke Screen" at the end of this article). But those concerns should not play a key role in the acquisition decision. The actual impact of tax and accounting treatments on value and its distribution is not as great as it may seem.

Shareholder Value at Risk (SVAR)

Before committing themselves to a major deal, both parties will, of course, need to assess the effect on each company's shareholder value should the synergy expectations embedded in the premium fail to materialize. In other words, what percentage of the company's market value are you betting on the success or failure of the acquisition? We present two simple tools for measuring synergy risk, one for the acquirer and the other for the seller.

A useful tool for assessing the relative magnitude of synergy risk for the acquirer is a straightforward calculation we call *shareholder value at risk*. SVAR is simply the premium paid for the acquisition divided by the market value of the acquiring company before the announcement is made. The index can also be calculated as the premium percentage multiplied by the market value of the seller relative to the market value of the buyer. (See "What Is an Acquirer's Risk in an All-Cash Deal?") We think of it as a "bet your company" index, which shows how much of your company's value is at risk if no postacquisition synergies are realized. The greater the premium percentage paid to sellers and the greater their market value relative to the acquiring company, the higher the SVAR. Of course, as we've seen, it's possible for acquirers to lose even more than their premium. In those cases, SVAR underestimates risk.

Let's see what the SVAR numbers are for our hypothetical deal. Buyer Inc. was proposing to pay a premium of $1.2 billion, and its own market value was $5 billion. In a cash deal, its SVAR would therefore be 1.2 divided by 5, or 24%. But if Seller Inc.'s shareholders are offered stock, Buyer Inc.'s SVAR decreases because some of the risk is transferred to the selling shareholders. To calculate Buyer Inc.'s SVAR for a stock deal, you must multiply the all-cash SVAR of 24% by the percentage that Buyer Inc. will own in the combined company, or 55.5%. Buyer Inc.'s SVAR for a stock deal is therefore just 13.3%.

A variation of SVAR—*premium at risk*—can help shareholders of a selling company assess their risks if the synergies don't materialize. The question for sellers is, What percentage of the premium is at risk in a stock offer? The answer is the percentage of ownership the seller will have in the combined company. In our hypothetical deal, therefore, the premium at risk for Seller Inc.'s shareholders is 44.5%. Once again, the premium-at-risk calculation is actually a rather conservative measure of risk, as it assumes that the value of the

---

What Is an Acquirer's Risk in an All-Cash Deal?

An acquirer's shareholder value at risk (SVAR) varies both with the relative size of the acquisition and the premium paid.

		RELATIVE SIZE OF THE SELLER TO THE ACQUIRER			
		.25	**.50**	**.75**	**1.00**
Premium	**30%**	7.5%	15%	22.5%	30%
	40%	10%	20%	30%	40%
	50%	12.5%	25%	37.5%	50%
	60%	15%	30%	45%	60%

Source: Alfred Rappaport, *Creating Shareholder Value: A Guide for Managers and Investors* (Free Press, 1998), p. 146.

SVAR and Premium at Risk for Major Stock Deals Announced in 1998

Acquirer	Seller	Premium	Relative Size of the Seller to the Acquirer	Cash SVAR	Acquirer's Proportional Ownership	Stock SVAR	Seller's Premium at Risk
McKesson-Robbins	HBO & Co.	30%	1.41	42%	37%	16%	63%
Tyco International	AMP	66%	0.18	12%	78%	9%	22%
Halliburton	Dresser Industries	15%	0.58	9%	60%	5%	40%
Household International	Beneficial	82%	1.01	83%	63%	52%	37%
Conseco	Green Tree Financial	83%	0.39	32%	60%	19%	40%
Office Depot	Viking Office Products	42%	0.63	26%	63%	16%	37%

Data for calculations courtesy of Securities Data Company. The cash SVAR percentage is calculated as the premium percentage multiplied by the relative size of the seller to the acquirer. The stock SVAR percentage is calculated as the cash SVAR percentage multiplied by the acquirer's proportional ownership.

independent businesses is safe and only the premium is at risk. But as Conseco's acquisition of Green Tree Financial demonstrates, unsuccessful deals can cost both parties more than just the premium. (See "SVAR and Premium at Risk for Major Stock Deals Announced in 1998.")

From the perspective of the selling company's shareholders, the premium-at-risk calculation highlights the attractiveness of a fixed-value offer relative to a fixed-share offer. Let's go back to our two companies. If Buyer Inc.'s stock price falls during the preclosing period by the entire premium paid, then Seller Inc.'s shareholders receive additional shares. Since no synergy expectations are built into the price of those shares now, Seller Inc.'s premium at risk has been completely absorbed by Buyer Inc. In other words, Seller Inc.'s shareholders receive not only more shares but also less risky shares. But in a fixed-share transaction, Seller Inc.'s stockholders have to bear their full share of the value lost through the fall in Buyer Inc.'s price right from the announcement date.

Although we have taken a cautionary tone in this article, we are not advocating that companies should always avoid using stock to pay for acquisitions. We have largely focused on deals that have taken place in established industries such as hotels and insurance. Stock issues are a natural way for young companies with limited access to other forms of financing, particularly in new industries, to pay for acquisitions. In those cases, a high stock valuation can be a major advantage.

Even managers of Internet companies like Amazon or Yahoo! Should not be beguiled into thinking that issuing stock is risk-free.

But it is a vulnerable one, and even the managers of Internet companies such as America Online, Amazon.com, and Yahoo! should not be beguiled into thinking that issuing stock is risk-free. Once the market has given a thumbs-down to one deal by marking down the acquirer's share price, it is likely to be more guarded about future deals. A poor stock-price performance can also undermine the motivation of employees and slow a company's momentum, making the difficult task of integrating acquisitions even harder. Worse, it can trigger a spiral of decline because companies whose share prices perform badly find it hard to attract and retain good people. Internet and other high-technology companies are especially vulnerable to this situation because they need to be able to offer expectations of large stock-option gains to recruit the best from a scarce pool of talent. The choice between cash and stock should never be made without full and careful consideration of the potential consequences. The all-too-frequent disappointing returns from stock transactions underscore how important it is for the boards of both parties to understand the ramifications and be vigilant on behalf of their shareholders' interests.

Why the Market Is Skeptical About Acquisitions

ONE THING ABOUT MERGERS and acquisitions has not changed since the 1980s. In about two-thirds of all acquisitions, the acquirer's stock price falls immediately after the deal is announced. In most cases, that drop is just a precursor of worse to come. The market's routinely negative response to M&A announcements reflects investors' skepticism about the likelihood that the acquirer will be able both to maintain the original values of the businesses in question and to achieve the synergies required to justify the premium. And the larger the premium, the worse the share-price performance. But why is the market so skeptical? Why do acquiring companies have such a difficult time creating value for their shareholders?

First of all, many acquisitions fail simply because they set too high a performance bar. Even without the acquisition premium, performance improvements have already been built into the prices of both the acquirer and the seller. Research has shown that the current level of operating performance accounts for only between 20% to 40% of a company's stock price. The rest is based entirely on expected improvements to current performance. The 30% to 40% premium typically paid for an acquisition therefore just adds to what is already a significant expectation for improvement. What's more, if important resources are diverted from some businesses during the integration process, performance gains from synergy can easily be canceled out by declines in the units providing the resources.

In other cases, acquisitions turn sour because the benefits they bring are easily replicated by competitors. Competitors will not stand idly by while an acquirer attempts to generate synergies at their expense. Arguably, acquisitions that do not confer a sustainable competitive advantage should not command any premium at all. Indeed, acquisitions may actually increase a company's vulnerability to competitive attack because the demands of integration can divert attention away from competitors. Acquisitions also create an opportunity for competitors to poach talent while organizational uncertainty is high. Take Deutsche Bank, for example. After it acquired Bankers Trust, Deutsche Bank had to pay huge sums to retain top-performing people in both organizations.

A third cause of problems is the fact that acquisitions—although a quick route to growth—require full payment up front. By contrast, investments in research and development, capacity expansion, or marketing campaigns can be made in stages over time. Thus in acquisitions, the financial clock starts ticking on the entire investment right from the beginning. Not unreasonably, investors want to see compelling evidence that timely performance gains will materialize. If they don't, they will mark the company's shares down before any integration takes place.

Fourth, all too often the purchase price of an acquisition is driven by the pricing of other "comparable" acquisitions rather than by a rigorous assessment of where, when, and how management can drive real performance gains. Thus the price paid may have little to do with achievable value. Finally, if a merger does go wrong, it is difficult and extremely expensive to unwind. Managers whose credibility is at stake in an acquisition may compound the value destroyed by throwing good money after bad in the hope that more time and money will prove them right.

Tax Consequences of Acquisitions

THE WAY AN ACQUISITION IS paid for affects the tax bills of the shareholders involved. On the face of it, a cash purchase of shares is the most tax-favorable way for the acquirer to make an acquisition because it offers the opportunity to revalue assets and thereby increase the depreciation expense for tax purposes. Conversely, shareholders in the selling company will face a tax bill for capital gains if they accept cash. They are therefore likely to bargain up the price to compensate for that cost, which may well offset the acquirer's tax benefits. But it's difficult to generalize. After all, if the selling shareholders suffer losses on their shares, or if their shares are in tax-exempt pension funds, they may favor cash rather than stock.

By contrast, the tax treatments for stock-financed acquisitions appear to favor the selling shareholders because they allow them to receive the acquirer's stock tax-free. In other words, selling shareholders can defer taxes until they sell the acquirer's stock. But if sellers are to realize the deferred tax benefit, they must be long-term shareholders and consequently must assume their full share of the postclosing synergy risk.

Accounting: Seeing Through the Smoke Screen

SOME MANAGERS CLAIM THAT stock deals are better for earnings than cash deals. But this focus on reported earnings flies in the face of economic sense and is purely a consequence of accounting convention.

In the United States, cash deals must be accounted for through the purchase-accounting method. This approach, which is widespread in the developed world, records the assets and liabilities of the acquired company at their fair market value and classifies the difference between the acquisition price and that fair value as goodwill. The goodwill must then be amortized, which causes a reduction in reported earnings after the merger is completed.

In contrast, acquisitions that are at least 90% paid for in shares, and meet a number of other requirements, can be accounted for under the pooling-of-interests method. This approach requires companies simply to combine their book values, creating no goodwill to be amortized. Therefore, better earnings results are reported. Perhaps not surprisingly, a recent proposal by the Financial Accounting Standards Board to eliminate pooling has caused deep consternation in corporate boardrooms concerned about earnings and among investment bankers who fear a serious downturn in M&A activity.

In principle, though, the accounting treatment should make no difference to an acquisition's value. Although it can dramatically affect the reported earnings of the acquiring company, it does not affect operating cash flows. Goodwill amortization is a noncash item and should not affect value. Managers are well aware of this, but many of them contend that investors are myopically addicted to short-term earnings and cannot see through the cosmetic differences between the two accounting methods.

Research evidence does not support that claim, however. Studies consistently show that the market does not reward companies for using pooling-of-interests accounting. Nor do goodwill charges from purchase accounting adversely affect stock prices. In fact, the market reacts more favorably to purchase transactions than to pooling transactions. The message for management is clear: value acquisitions on the basis of their economic substance—their future cash flows—not on the basis of short-term earnings generated by accounting conventions.

Originally published in Novemver–December 1999
Reprint 99611

Can This Merger Be Saved?

SARAH CLIFFE

Executive Summary

IN THIS FICTIONAL CASE STUDY, a merger that looked like a marriage made in heaven to those at corporate headquarters is feeling like an infernal union to those on the ground.

The merger is between Synergon Capital, a U.S. financial-services behemoth, and Beauchamp, Becker & Company, a venerable British financial-services company with strong profits and an extraordinarily loyal client base of wealthy individuals. Beauchamp also boasts a strong group of senior managers led by Julian Mansfield, a highly cultured and beloved patriarch who personifies all that's good about the company.

Synergon isn't accustomed to acquiring such companies. It usually encircles a poorly managed turnaround candidate and then, once the deal is done, drops a neutron bomb on it, leaving file cabinets and contracts but no people. Before acquiring Beauchamp, Synergon's macho men offered loud assurances that they would leave the tradition-bound company alone—provided, of course, that Beauchamp met the ambitious target numbers and showed sufficient enthusiasm for cross-selling Synergon's products to its wealthy clients.

In charge of making the acquisition work is Nick Cunningham, one of Synergon's more thoughtful executives. Nick, who was against the deal from the start, is the face and voice of Synergon for Julian Mansfield. And Mansfield, in his restrained way, is angry at the constant flow of bureaucratic forms, at the rude demands for instant information, at the peremptory changes. He's even dropping broad hints at retirement. Nick has already been warned: if Mansfield goes, you go.

Six commentators advise Nick on how to save his job by bringing peace and prosperity to the feuding couple.

Nᴉᴄᴋ ᴄᴜɴɴɪɴɢʜᴀᴍ ʜᴀᴅ ʙᴇᴇɴ against the Beauchamp acquisition from the beginning. Nick's company, Synergon Capital, was a U.S. financial-services behemoth, constantly on the lookout for acquisitions. Typically it acquired turnaround candidates—small companies with established market positions and poor management. But Beauchamp, Becker & Company—a British financial-services company with a great history, strong profits, and an extraordinarily loyal client base of wealthy individuals—didn't fit that description at all.

Nick told his boss, J.J. d'Amato, exactly what he thought. "We'll have to pay too much," he said. "And our cultures are completely different. We don't play the same game. They don't care at all about growth."

J.J. scoffed. "Stop being such a wuss. Let's just do it. I'm sure we can find some money they're leaving on the table." J.J. was rising fast in the company. Listening to subordinates was not among his strengths.

"I'm not so sure," responded Nick. "This isn't a dog that no one wants, run by amateurs. They know more about their customers than we ever will. They're different."

"You worry too much about the soft stuff, Nick," J.J. said. "Relax. We won't force them to change that much. You'll figure out how to make the numbers."

The Synergon Style

Nick had been with Synergon for three years. He'd signed on because of the company's powerhouse performance. Synergon's acquisitions style was legendary. It used a crack team of financial auditors and operations professionals in the due diligence phase to figure out where it could add value. Every team had a "war room" at corporate headquarters with charts, fax machines, computers, and phones. It was staffed around the clock until the deal was done. The team prided itself on identifying every nickel the target business took in or spent.

After Synergon closed a deal, its integration machinery took over. Within weeks, it would close the acquired company's back-office operations and shift work to the nearest Synergon office. Since the acquired company was usually badly managed, Synergon would fire most of the management team within 12 months. Internally, they called this tactic "neutron bombing." The people were gone; only file drawers and contracts remained.

Synergon relished its rough culture. Due diligence teams were called "commando squads"; its members got 18-inch bowie knives with their names and that of the acquired business engraved on them. Negotiating teams got silver-plated sledgehammers if they closed a deal at a price lower than the figure initially quoted to the board. Operating managers who achieved an acquired business's earnings and productivity targets in the first year got 12-inch-long models of a piranha.

Synergon's CEO swore that a "take no prisoners" approach was vital to survival. "The marketplace is war," he told new M.B.A. recruits. "That nickel you see at the end of the negotiation table belongs to us. Get it. It's ours. There may be some collateral damage along the way, but it's our damn nickel."

Sometimes Nick found himself at odds with this culture. It's not that he wasn't competitive, but he had a more thoughtful side than many of his colleagues. He was worried that the Synergon style would someday get in its own way when the company was faced with a situation that didn't fit into its game plan. And Beauchamp, it seemed to him, might be that situation.

A Marriage Made in Heaven

Still, the acquisition made sense. Beauchamp would give Synergon a foothold in Europe—a key part of the company's strategic plan—as well as access to extremely desirable customers. And the deal could make sense from Beauchamp's point of view, too. The company needed to grow, and Synergon had deep pockets, plus some areas of expertise that Beauchamp lacked.

But the acquisition made Nick nervous because it would only work under two conditions: first, if Beauchamp's customers remained happy and, second, if Julian Mansfield, Beauchamp's longtime managing director, stayed on board. Mansfield was smart, sophisticated, and polished. Synergon could learn a lot from how Mansfield managed his clients. The problem was, Synergon didn't think in terms of learning.

Nick pointed out this problem one last time before J.J.'s acquisition pitch to the board, but to no avail. "Let it go, Nick. We're going to jam this through and they're going to love it."

And J.J. was masterful before the board. "We will leave Beauchamp alone. It's a great cross-selling opportunity for us," he said, looking deferentially at Synergon's CEO, Norman Waskewich. "And Nick will help get them focused on growth."

J.J. was on a roll. "Synergon's management and Beauchamp's customers. It's a home run. A slam dunk. They will learn what we've always known: You have to grow or die. They will grow."

Right after the meeting, J.J. set the rules. Pointing a finger directly at Nick, he said, "You have three tasks. One, Beauchamp doubles its earnings in three years. They need a 20% pop in income in year one. Cut some heads and we'll get there. Two, no blowups at Beauchamp. Nada. The press and the analysts are all over us on this deal. Third, I want their big customers so I can pitch our products. And I want Mansfield to get me in. If he walks, they walk, and our pitch walks. If Mansfield walks, you walk out right behind him. Got it?"

The Venerable Beauchamp

Soon after the deal closed, Nick made a quick trip to London. He met briefly with Julian Mansfield and the rest of the senior management team. There was a lot of polite talk about Beauchamp's wonderful traditions and the "significant synergies" that existed between the two companies, but not much of substance occurred.

Nick scheduled a second trip for a month later—he was facing the end of Synergon's fiscal year and couldn't get back any sooner. In spare moments during the ensuing weeks, he studied Beauchamp. The place was impressive, no doubt about it. Beauchamp was an unusually stable company. Its management team consisted of 16 people who'd worked together for more than a decade. The 700 associates routinely shifted from one project team to another to handle a surge in business, solve a customer problem, or get a product to market. The turnover rate was a mere 4%, and managers averaged 21 years of experience with the company. (In contrast, Synergon's turnover rate was 21%, and the average tenure for managers was 6 years.)

Julian Mansfield presided over the whole like an old-fashioned patriarch. His title was managing director, but he *was* Beauchamp. He was the godfather of dozens of associates' children. He was revered within the company for his business sense and character, and he was well known in charity circles for his generosity.

As Nick was pondering his second face-to-face meeting with Mansfield, the Synergon integration team swung into action. First, Synergon's HR director informed his counterpart at Beauchamp that Beauchamp's Associate Bonus Plan, which provided every associate with at least a modest bonus, would be scrapped. Synergon's Big Bang Bonus Plan, which favored senior managers who achieved high earnings growth, would take its place. The change would reduce the bonus for 70% of Beauchamp's associates.

Second, Synergon closed the cafeteria that for years had provided Beauchamp employees with a free lunch. Employees complained to one another as they ran out at lunchtime for take-out food. Julian was mortified that the "caf ladies," who'd been with Beauchamp for years, were let go with only a minimal severance package.

Third, Synergon's finance director informed his counterpart that purchasing and travel would now go through Synergon vendors. Agreements with vendors in these areas were geared toward big-ticket items, such as executive office furniture or cross-Atlantic airfare. Although Synergon's arrangements kept its own costs down, they were bound to push Beauchamp's up, since the smaller firm used regional carriers with lower local fares. People at Beauchamp were upset that long-standing relationships with local suppliers would be eliminated.

To top it all off, Synergon was now requiring multiple approvals before granting customer credit; the approvals would be based on customer industry, contract profitability, customer location, and the type of asset offered as collateral. Beauchamp salespeople had always made credit decisions with a conversation and a handshake. Under the new regime, Beauchamp received its first customer complaint in living memory when a valued customer of many years lost a deal while waiting for his loan approval to come through.

Julian and his longtime executive assistant, Olivia Carlton, heard daily complaints, too, about the new reports and forms that Beauchamp managers had to fill out for Synergon officials, who never introduced themselves or explained why the forms were necessary. Synergon was asking for numbers on market share, competitor data, cost reductions, productivity increases, and risk allocation.

When direct communication did take place, it was horrible. The day before Nick's second visit, a Synergon financial auditor brought Olivia to tears. "Fax me the F-14 sheet in the next hour or I will be in your face Monday morning and your boss will hear about it. *Get me my report.*"

The Honeymoon's Over

When Nick walked into Julian's office on his second visit, the older man rose and shook hands, trying to be cordial, but he was clearly annoyed. After some initial small talk, he said to Nick, "Let me ask you a question. Is Synergon *trying* to offend me?"

"Goodness, no," said Nick, taken aback. "What do you mean?"

"Well, you can see that I'm not a small man," answered Julian. (Indeed, he was well over six feet tall.) "As you know, I travel a great deal, and I happen to suffer from arthritis. Yet my assistant has just informed me that I'm not to fly business class to Paris. Company policy doesn't *allow* that without permission from my superior. That would be you, I expect...?"

Nick stuttered out an explanation and assured Julian that the policy would be overridden. Julian gazed out the window for a long moment, then turned back to Nick.

"Look, Mr. Cunningham, we can help you reach these absurdly high target numbers you've set, but not unless you let us do our work."

"What do you mean?" responded Nick, genuinely puzzled.

"I'll show you what I mean," said Julian, opening his desk drawer and pulling out a two-inch pile of faxes. "These are just a few of the vital, urgent, ASAP messages we've received from your people. Do you have any idea how time-consuming and idiotic these forms are?"

Nick recognized most of them. Some were administrative: the travel center asking whether the "new employee" would prefer nonsmoking hotel rooms and what kind of airplane seat, aisle or window.

Some were procedural: HR asking that performance evaluations be completed for all subordinates in SEPR format—which meant Synergon Employee Performance Review, but there was no explanation. And the S-EEO-1, which asked Beauchamp to classify employees by race, gender, and level, something not done in the United Kingdom.

Some were financial: the B-52s, growth projections for the next three years, and the M-16s, cost-reduction sheets for the past 12 months.

All told, several dozen requests from 14 different people at corporate. Nick recognized this as routine work that Synergon managers did at home on Sunday afternoons.

"I'll do my best," replied Nick. "I can get someone over here to help you out. But this is how we operate."

Mansfield narrowed his eyes and said with barely concealed anger, "I'm sure it is how you operate. But if your operations mean that my company—which was ticking along very nicely, thank you—becomes paralyzed, then we both have a problem. You people have a very odd notion of what 'leaving Beauchamp alone' means."

After a brief pause, he went on. "You know, Mr. Cunningham, you seem like a nice fellow. But I've been around too long to have to put up with this much impertinence. To have these boys you call auditors insulting my assistant is, frankly, something I can do without. My wife's been on at me to retire for the last year or two and, I must say, that idea is starting to sound attractive.

"I have a suggestion. Why don't you take the rest of the day off? You can get over your jet lag. There's a Sargent exhibition at the Tate that you might enjoy, and Miss Carlton could probably get you some theater tickets for tonight, if you like. Why don't we meet tomorrow morning, after you've slept on it, to talk about the future of the company."

Can the Beauchamp acquisition be salvaged? How should Nick prepare for tomorrow's meeting with Julian?

Six commentators explain how Nick can bring peace and prosperity to the newly merged companies.

> **BILL PAUL** *is a partner in DelTech Consulting, a firm that specializes in acquisitions integration. It is based in Avon, Connecticut.*

Nick Cunningham's problem is that Synergon excels at assimilating new companies but is terrible at integrating them. Between the two tasks lies a world of difference.

Assimilation works when the goal of the acquisition is to consolidate the two companies. In such cases, the deal itself is the major work. Once the deal has gone through, the objective is simple: make the acquired company just like the purchaser. In some cases, a consolidating acquisition means isolating a tangible asset, product line, or high-performing unit and forgetting the rest. In any event, the acquired company's organizational culture doesn't matter, because it likely caused the underperformance that led to the acquisition. The same is true for that company's people. Their only choice is to adapt or leave.

Assimilation does not work in the case of a strategic acquisition, joint venture, or merger—integration is required instead. The real work begins after the deal. The goal is either to create a wholly new third company or to maintain separate identities while sharing strengths. The acquired company changes some practices, keeps others, and transfers still others to the purchaser. Organizational culture is critical, and people are paramount—the purchaser should retain most of the acquired company's employees.

Acquiring organizations are inclined to force assimilation on their new companies, regardless of circumstances. After a deal, many well-intentioned people will inundate the acquired company with requests and changes in an attempt to improve its business performance or its connections with the new parent. The result is an "accumulation effect" in which each request is modest in its own right, but the totality paralyzes the acquisition. Over time, this effect erodes the behaviors that made the company a success. That's exactly what is happening in this case. Beauchamp requires integration, and Nick needs to override Synergon's usual assimilation tactics.

In the short term, Nick should appoint an on-site integration manager from Synergon. Beauchamp doesn't know who or what is important, so every request appears serious, even the F-14 sheet from the financial auditor, who may be a first-year associate trying to impress the bosses. Beauchamp has no idea whether the form needs attention today or next week—or perhaps it can be stored in the circular file? The Synergon integration manager would know.

Nick then needs to drive a strategy that applies the three C's of integration: clarity, conflict resolution, and consensus building.

Nick must identify and clarify the "nonnegotiables" of the deal. Those are mainly the financial targets that led Synergon to make the acquisition. They include increasing Beauchamp's net income by 20% in the first year, doubling it in three years, and reducing the head count. Other nonnegotiables would include adhering to Synergon's risk-assessment process and introducing Beauchamp's customers to Synergon.

Nick also needs to clarify the differences between the businesses and why those differences exist. When you tamper with a business without understanding why it is successful, you confuse people in the acquired company and risk destroying its value. When two organizations are of equal size, such misunderstanding results in cultural wars that make it impossible to realize financial goals; consider the deal involving AT&T and NCR. And if the purchaser is much larger, the acquired company's strengths are usually trampled on. That's what happened when Quaker Oats bought Snapple, and that's what's happening in this case.

Nick can still prevent the misunderstandings from ending in disaster. To build consensus, he should bring the key people from both sides together for a couple of days. In-depth discussions will allow the two companies' executives to gain an appreciation of their different places in the market and different approaches to doing business. Having done that, the two sides should come to an understanding—based on available data and customer research—about what the market demands are likely to be over the next couple of years. If Synergon and Beauchamp build a business model based on the connections between market demands, competitive advantages, and organizational processes, they will be able to resolve organizational conflicts.

This group meeting is essential. If Nick fails to bring the two sides together around market demands, people will try to resolve problems one at a time, the integration process will drag on, and the acquisition will suffer. In another scenario, conflicts will simply be resolved on the basis of power or politics. In other words, Synergon will win every battle but destroy the reason for the deal.

Nick needs to get Mansfield on his side. He needs to express regret about how the transition has gone so far.

Once a broad consensus has been reached, it will be possible for Julian Mansfield to talk about specific difficulties. For example, he may contend that Beauchamp will not be able to double its net income in three years *and* abide by Synergon's risk process. The reason? Competitors will poach customers by offering a quick turnaround on financing. Synergon's managers may disagree, but at least the two sides will be able to have a reasonable discussion.

One last note: before any of this can work, Nick needs to get Mansfield on his side. He needs to empathize with him and express personal regret about how the transition process has gone so far. In return, he needs a commitment from Mansfield that he will stay on and help Nick with the transition. If these two men can begin to understand each other, they may be able to salvage the acquisition.

J. BRAD MCGEE *is a senior vice president at Tyco International, the conglomerate based in Exeter, New Hampshire.*

"Our assets wear shoes." I first heard that expression from the CEO of a service-based company while I was in the diligence phase of acquiring her business. She was referring to the people-oriented nature of service companies—their reliance on relationships and the unique skills of individuals. In this case, she was advising me to be cautious about unraveling the fabric that held her people together. The same cautionary words apply to Synergon's acquisition of Beauchamp.

Clearly, this acquisition is a departure for Synergon. Its success depends not solely on reducing costs but also on increasing revenues. That's difficult for two reasons. First, selling incremental products to the same customers requires that they change their behavior. Second, it's hard to forecast increased revenues accurately; forecasts in this case would be susceptible to exaggeration. Nonetheless, this acquisition can be saved.

I've been involved in dozens of acquisitions, and in my experience there's always room for improvement—even when a company is well managed. I recommend that Nick do the following:

Make Julian Mansfield part of the solution, not the problem. Mansfield has already expressed his willingness to help Synergon reach its "absurdly high" target numbers. At least for the short term, Nick should leave Mansfield clearly in charge of Beauchamp and allow him to create and own the plan to realize Synergon's targets. He likely performed his own diligence on Synergon before the merger and understood their financial goals. He also likely gave his blessing to the merger knowing that he would be under Synergon's management.

Put Mansfield on an attractive P&L-based incentive program. If Mansfield is a good manager, he will use the new tools available to him to drive both revenue gains and cost reductions based on the aggressive P&L targets. Those tools include access to a broader range of products and to Synergon's ideas about streamlining operations. Large cost-reduction opportunities can exist even in well-managed companies that are acquired. A well-structured incentive plan could be all Beauchamp needs. At the end of the day, does it matter how Mansfield achieves the targets?

Put a finance person from Synergon into Beauchamp. Make sure that the CFO or corporate controller at Beauchamp is a person who knows Synergon. The importance of this action cannot be overstated. Having such a person in place offers two advantages: it establishes an insider who can monitor Beauchamp's financial health, its progress toward meeting goals, and its organizational dynamics; and it gives Mansfield direct access to knowledge about how he should be integrating the two firms. Finance people often work well in this role. They are generally viewed as nonthreatening and often have a good understanding of business operations.

Closely monitor Mansfield's performance. Due diligence can be very good at identifying the financial, legal, and environmental fitness of an acquisition target. However, it often fails to uncover the interpersonal dynamics that hold service companies together. In this case, it's difficult to assess how critical Mansfield is to Beauchamp's continued success. Nick should use the first three to six months after the merger as an evaluation period (the finance person is critical to this phase). After that, it should be clear whether or not Synergon needs to keep Mansfield on board.

Back off the bureaucracy. Synergon's bureaucracy will only burden Beauchamp, and it may prove demoralizing.

Now to the more immediate concern in this case: the upcoming meeting between Nick and Julian. Nick should brief J.J. d'Amato on the plan of action detailed above and have d'Amato recommend a financial person to bring into Beauchamp. Nick should think through the plan

> *During the meeting, Nick must get Mansfield to agree to include a Synergon financial person on his management team.*

and be able to discuss it clearly and provide supporting arguments for each part of the plan.

During the meeting, he should assure Mansfield that he will be in charge of achieving the aggressive targets for Beauchamp and that he will be enriched for meeting or exceeding those goals. At the same time, he must inform Mansfield of the ways Synergon can help him, and he must get Mansfield to agree to include a Synergon financial person on his management team.

The meetings I've had of this type have gone very smoothly. Although people are often reluctant to change, they also realize—whether they say so or not—that being acquired means relinquishing ownership and control of their company.

JILL GREENTHAL *is a managing director of Donaldson, Lufkin, and Jenrette in New York City. She was the lead investment banker for TCI in its merger with AT&T.*

The senior management team at Synergon knew that they needed to "leave Beauchamp alone." But somehow that idea was forgotten after the deal went through. Nick's task now is to build a constituency within Synergon to treat the Beauchamp acquisition differently. It won't be easy, because Synergon's leaders have a playbook approach to acquisitions, and they've been very successful with it. This time, though, they've bought a good business, not a broken one, and they need to recognize that.

They also need to recognize—through actions, not lip service—that they've bought a company driven by the personality of its senior managers, especially Julian Mansfield. The problem is, Beauchamp's senior people probably made a fair amount of money from the sale, and it's going to be hard for Synergon to enlist the aid and support of people it's just made financially comfortable. Many acquiring companies recognize this problem in the deal structure and pay senior management over two to three years, as goals are met. If Synergon has failed to consider this issue, it should move fast and put in place some very large incentives to get Mansfield and members of his senior management team to stay.

Next, Synergon needs to rethink the mechanics of integration. It can't leave Beauchamp completely alone, but neither should it take over every aspect of the business. It has to find a balance. For example, Synergon has a legal responsibility to understand Beauchamp's numbers, its financial reporting, and its credit risks. But other areas, such as purchasing and employee benefits, can be left to Beauchamp's discretion. Matters aren't helped by the condescending attitude drifting across the Atlantic from corporate headquarters. That attitude indicates that Synergon believes it has taken on another broken company and is prepared to demolish the old structure and build an entirely new one.

So far, Nick hasn't really done his job. There are, however, several steps he can take to avert a meltdown.

Essentially, Nick must serve as—or appoint—a referee who will make the integration work by helping the two companies understand each other.

To accomplish that goal, he needs to persuade people on both sides to think in new ways. He must convince the people at Synergon headquarters that the acquisition will fail unless certain rules are broken—that, for example, not *all* the company's forms are critical to Beauchamp's future success. And he needs to be Mansfield's advocate at the top levels of the company. He's the only one who can absorb Mansfield's concerns and translate them effectively.

In the meantime, he should reassure Mansfield at their next meeting that he will work on Beauchamp's behalf to reduce the bureaucratic irritations now plaguing the company. Then he should turn to the serious matter of making the numbers. It's a hopeful sign that Mansfield seems to understand the objectives and has even indicated that Beauchamp can meet Synergon's "absurdly high" target numbers.

It's critical that Mansfield agree to cross-sell Synergon's products. That's not going to happen unless it's in the financial interests of Beauchamp's associates, including Mansfield. Nick and Julian need to map out a sound game plan that includes changes in compensation, cross-selling incentives, and an understanding about how to retain customers and employees. If Beauchamp's employees have not been granted stock in Synergon, that omission should be corrected.

During these conversations, it will be important for Nick to convey to Mansfield what he needs to do to become part of the corporate team. At the same time, they need to start planning for Mansfield's eventual retirement. Should they look to the next layer at

Beauchamp? Or should they bring people in from Synergon to learn the business? This issue needs to be addressed sooner rather than later.

If Nick can persuade Synergon's top management not to fix what ain't broke, and if he can hold Mansfield's hand a little while the integration phase moves forward, then Beauchamp's future has a chance to be a happy marriage of growth and tradition.

DALE MATSCHULLAT *is vice president and general counsel for Newell Company in Freeport, Illinois; he oversees the company's acquisition integrations.*

In my experience, it is easier to do a job yourself than to manage others who are trying to do it. The Synergon story suggests that my experience is valid.

If I were meeting with Julian Mansfield, I would start by telling him that I appreciate his signing on to Synergon's budgetary goals. I would let him know that, although we must agree on budgetary and strategic goals, he will ultimately be in charge of reaching them.

Next, I would ask Mansfield to develop a strategic plan for the business. The plan should be reviewed at least annually and must include: an analysis of the marketplace; an assessment of competitors' strengths and a plan for exploiting their weaknesses; suggestions for building on Beauchamp's strengths and attacking its weaknesses; a discussion of strategic opportunities; and a plan to make cross-selling effective. The strategic plan should contain virtually no numbers.

I would also ask Mansfield to prepare a budget for the next operating year—a nuts-and-bolts document that commits the company to figures for sales and profits. It will be negotiated with me and others at Synergon and must be based on a realistic sales forecast. Once the terms have been agreed on, they have to be met.

It is important that Mansfield's team develop these documents. As long as Mansfield can sell his vision to Synergon, he will shape the future of Beauchamp. Synergon has the capital to make his vision real.

Further, I would discuss the huge dissonance between the corporate cultures. I would tell Mansfield that I am going to bring a high-level Synergon manager into Beauchamp—probably a corporate controller. The controller, who will be a member of Beauchamp's senior management team, will handle inside operations and manage costs. Mansfield will be free to manage sales growth and customer relationships. He and the controller will meld the two cultures.

All those ASAP messages from Synergon will go directly to the new controller. If there are problems, I would tell Mansfield this: "Not only will I be your boss, I will be your shield. You are responsible for Beauchamp's success, and as long as you respond successfully, you will be left to run it. It is my job to see to that."

I would then focus on Mansfield's hints about retirement. Optimally, Mansfield should run Beauchamp. But it is unacceptable for him to manage the integration with his mind on retirement. I would remind him that Synergon paid a premium for Beauchamp, partly because of its respect for his accomplishments. Synergon believes that he has the vision, guts, experience, and stamina to grow the company. However, unless Mansfield is 100% behind the endeavor, Synergon will not provide the capital he needs to do it.

Mansfield has to understand that Synergon, in its brash way, brings important principles to the table. It is very profit oriented and believes in lean, decentralized organizations that are self-driven but accountable.

So if Mansfield wants to fly business class around Europe, I will support it. But his strategic plan is going to require substantial growth. Perhaps he would prefer to fly coach and spend the savings on another design engineer. Such trade-offs are his to make, but he is accountable.

And yes, we can phase in the Synergon bonus plan. But at Synergon, bonuses are an important part of the compensation scheme. They are awarded when the budgeted numbers have been achieved. They are not given out for *any* other reason. Mansfield will have to find a way to motivate Beauchamp's midlevel associates without a bonus plan.

If Mansfield agrees to implement the ideas outlined in this meeting, Synergon will have purchased Beauchamp on the cheap.

DANIEL VASELLA *is president of Novartis, the company that resulted from the merger of Ciba Geigy and Sandoz. It is based in Basel, Switzerland.*

Nick's not in an easy position. He has to manage a merger he doesn't believe in. His supervisor either does not understand or does not care about the cultural issues separating the companies being merged. And he's overseeing an acquired company whose managing director has been highly successful, is close to retirement, and has no incentive to change.

Nick has two choices. He can impose Synergon's culture—its strategy, business processes, and people—on Beauchamp. Or he can help Julian Mansfield find a way to operate in a reasonable environment. The first choice isn't really viable: Mansfield will leave, Nick will be fired, and the acquisition will fail. So Nick needs to ensure that he and Mansfield come to an understanding.

Nick should go into tomorrow's meeting with a crisis-management mind-set. He must stabilize the situation. He needs to get Mansfield's agreement to corrective actions, as well as his commitment to stay for at least six months. I suggest six months because I don't believe Mansfield would commit to staying longer at this stage. Once Nick has established that he's acting in good faith, he may be able to negotiate a longer-term commitment with Mansfield at a later date.

I propose that he do the following. First, he needs to recognize the tremendous past achievements of Mansfield and Beauchamp and establish a sense of mutual respect. Second, he needs to depict in a compelling way Beauchamp's opportunity to become Synergon's flagship European operation. Mansfield has to buy in to a common future that is better in some ways than Beauchamp's past. Third, Nick has to explain Synergon's original motives for the acquisition—not only to get a foothold in Europe but also to introduce Synergon's products to Beauchamp's customers. I'm not sure that Mansfield ever understood these things. Fourth, Nick must acknowledge the existing problems and his own responsibility for them. He should find out which problems are the most disturbing and require immediate correction, and how Mansfield would go about mending these problems. That is, Nick needs to tap Julian's experience and, in so doing, acknowledge his capabilities. It's important that he act quickly.

Further, Nick should talk not just with J.J. d'Amato but also with Synergon's CEO. This is a major acquisition; there's a lot of money at stake. He should request formal approval for corrective actions. For example, there should be a commitment that all requests from the United States be cleared through him. And if Julian has never met Synergon's CEO, Nick should arrange a meeting.

Finally, to tie up the loose ends of the short-term crisis, Nick should propose biweekly progress reviews, to be conducted either by phone or in person. The sum of these steps should prevent the short-term problems from leading to a total deterioration of the acquisition.

In the long term, you're left with the question of how you align two companies with totally different cultures. For example, I do not think that Beauchamp is well suited to grow Synergon in Europe. I would rather relocate one or two Synergon people and put them under Mansfield; they would be responsible for growing the business externally.

What are the lessons of this case? When you make an acquisition, you must have total agreement on the merger objectives and key strategies. You must share a vision of the value added by the merger. You have to be aware of cultural differences. Eventually, the customer base, the strategy, and the culture of the acquired company have to fit. And once you have a common understanding of the merger objectives and key strategies, you have to gain rapid agreement on responsibilities, accountability, empowerment, and boundaries—and you have to keep the lines of communication open.

ALBERT J. VISCIO *is a vice president of Booz·Allen & Hamilton in San Francisco. He has consulted extensively on postmerger integration.*

Synergon has made errors in both the mechanical integration and the strategic value integration of its new acquisition.

The mechanical integration is not being tailored to the situation. Instead, Synergon is using its standard integration process. Some of J.J. d'Amato's guidance has turned out to be just plain wrong. Cutting heads backfired. And the efficiencies being introduced aren't really efficiencies—Beauchamp's spending more on the airlines, for example.

Nobody ever clarified what "leaving Beauchamp alone" meant. It was Nick's job to do that. It was misleading to say "We'll leave you alone" and then close the cafeteria. Beauchamp didn't *feel* left alone. Synergon has created a very poor foundation for any kind of strategic integration.

This acquisition was about adding strategic value to both firms; it wasn't about cost reductions. But nobody seems to be talking about how strategic value will be added—and it doesn't happen automatically. Nick needs an answer to the question, What will the Synergon-owned Beauchamp look like? It's apparent that there is potential—Beauchamp needs to grow and Synergon wants wealthy European customers. But those mutual needs don't seem to be a focus of the integration effort. They should be. They're the whole point.

Nobody seems to be talking about how strategic value will be added—and it doesn't happen automatically.

Three elements have been lacking: vision, architecture, and leadership.

Synergon never developed a vision of what Beauchamp could be. The old model wasn't right: Beauchamp wasn't growing. Pulling it into the Synergon fold isn't working either. Nobody's put forth a new value proposition for customers. Without that, you don't have a company.

As far as we know, nobody's talked about architecture: How does Beauchamp fit into Synergon? How are the companies related? What's the process for cross-selling going to be? Synergon's tried-and-true integration mechanisms need to be tailored, probably radically.

Finally, Nick has abdicated his leadership responsibilities. He should have been working with Mansfield and the other Beauchamp senior managers on creating a shared vision and common values. But he hasn't spent much time on the ground with these people. They've been bothered with forms but not graced with his physical presence. Nick should be identifying and building leadership prospects from within Beauchamp's ranks—forming partnerships and building excitement about the company's future.

So Nick has a big problem: a derailed acquisition. He should go to that show tonight. Then he should find a way to reach common ground on a vision that will excite both Mansfield and Synergon's CEO. He needs to develop a process for getting there based on the understanding that value is going to be found in the market, not in cost savings.

He needs to find people at Beauchamp who will help lead that change process, and he probably needs to do battle with his own management. It's important that he talk to Mansfield and take responsibility for the many problems that have hurt the acquisition.

Having said all this, I have to point out that when a deal's success is contingent on retaining a senior person, it usually fails. We've done some research in order to understand why, and the answer is quite straightforward. When we asked top people why they'd moved on after a merger, they said, very simply, that they had no reason to stay.

Let's face it: when you acquire a company and neutron bomb it, you don't risk much because you don't need its people. But if the company's value lies in its customer relationships, you have to keep your finger off the button and think instead about the harder process of persuading the people you've acquired to work toward the company's goals.

Originally published in January–February 1999
Reprint 99103

Who Goes, Who Stays?

DAVID A. LIGHT

Executive Summary

THE MERGER ANNOUNCEMENT between DeWaal Pharmaceuticals and BioHealth Labs was front-page news. Pictures of CEO Steve Lindell and chairman Kaspar van de Velde had appeared in newspapers around the world. Two months later, the press had moved on to a new story, and the hard labor of integration loomed.

Steve had worked tirelessly to clear regulatory hurdles, and all signs pointed toward approval in the near future. Now Steve was feeling pressure to attack the real challenge of the merger: bringing together two very different cultures as quickly and efficiently as possible. DeWaal was an established drugmaker based in the Netherlands, and BioHealth, headquartered just north of New York City, had in recent years become competitive at the highest tier of the market. The first step in integrating the two companies was to select the top layers of management for the new company. At the moment, there were some 120 people on two continents for about 65 senior-level jobs.

Steve's urgency was not without cause: talented people from both sides were jumping ship, and Bio-Health's stock price had dipped 20% after the initial euphoria over the deal had worn off. Complicating matters was confusion over who was really in charge: Steve wanted to take leadership and move ahead rapidly, but he was often disarmed by Kaspar's charming persuasiveness. As the two men attempt to work through the important personnel issues during a lunch meeting, they quickly hit a roadblock. How can they come to agreement about who goes and who stays?

Four commentators offer advice in response to this fictional case.

THE MERGER ANNOUNCEMENT between DeWaal Pharmaceuticals and BioHealth Labs was front-page, top-of-the-hour news. Pictures of CEO Steve Lindell and chairman Kaspar van de Velde, beaming at each other like long-lost friends at a college reunion, had appeared in newspapers around the world. DeWaal, based in the Netherlands, was an established European drugmaker, and BioHealth, headquartered just north of New York City, had in recent years become competitive at the highest tier of the market. Both companies made and sold a wide range of drugs, from over-the-counter pain relievers to AIDS medications. The new mega-company, DeWaal BioHealth, would reap the benefits of scale: it would consolidate plants and staff while having more products to push through its distribution channels. Global headquarters would be in New York, but European manufacturing and sales would continue to be directed from Rotterdam. The new company's combined revenues were projected to top $8 billion.

Now, two months later, the TV cameras had moved on to a new story, and the hard labor of integration loomed. Ever since the announcement, Steve had worked tirelessly on clearing the regulatory hurdles presented by the FTC and the European Commission. And he noted with a mixture of satisfaction and relief that all signs pointed toward approval in the near future.

Yet Steve knew that the anticipated victory would be just the beginning of the game. The real challenge would lie in bringing together two very different cultures as quickly and efficiently as possible. He had to get the new company moving, and the first hurdle—it looked more like a pole vault to Steve—was selecting the top layers of management. At the moment, there were some 120 people on two continents for about 65 senior-level jobs.

Steve drained his third cup of coffee of the morning and checked his watch. Already 11 AM. He'd been at the office since 6:30 and in meetings for the past three hours. Now he had an hour to prepare for his meeting with Kaspar at one of New York's finest restaurants. Steve had suggested the company cafeteria, but Kaspar had cajoled him into making the drive to the city by invoking "the need to maintain a civilized life in this frantic world of ours." The meeting's agenda consisted of one item: deciding who would fill the high-level management posts.

The Exodus

As Steve gathered up the mass of papers he would need and stuffed them into his briefcase, there was a knock on his half-open door. Alison Whitney poked her head in and said, "Hey—got a minute?"

Alison was BioHealth's director of sales and marketing. She had shot into that position a year ago, at age 33, after establishing herself as the company's best sales rep. She had an easy, bantering relationship with Steve and was known for having her finger on the organization's pulse.

"I'm just out the door. What's up?"

"Yeah, I know, I know. You're meeting with Kaspar— that's what I need to talk with you about. I'll keep it brief."

"Fire away."

"I just have to let you know, before you make any final decisions about people, that everyone, and I mean everyone, here at corporate is terrified. Right or wrong, they think Kaspar is calling the shots. We've already lost, what, five people? And I can tell you, without naming names, that I know of three or four others who are weighing serious offers right now. Like I said, I had to let you know."

This wasn't the first time Steve had heard that people were confused about who was in charge. The question had already been raised by a handful of Wall Street analysts and a *BusinessWeek* reporter. The confusion puzzled and irritated Steve. He was, after all, the leader of the bigger organization and the new company's CEO— end of story. True, Kaspar had lost none of the drive and charisma that had made him one of Europe's most respected CEOs, but he was 62 and widely presumed to be on the road to retirement. That's why he had agreed to the position of chairman, Steve figured. But Kaspar, with his ability to charm the media, seemed to be creating the perception that he had more say in key decisions facing the new company than Steve.

The two men had worked well together during the merger negotiations. They had carefully traded off the positions at the very top of the new organization. Kaspar had insisted on having his people lead HR, operations in Europe, and global marketing; Steve, in return, had held out for COO, CFO, and head of R&D. Overall, Steve had been happy with the horse trading. The reports of tension between the two were based only on rumors, but Steve knew rumors could sometimes become facts if they are not quickly dispelled. All this flashed through his mind as he faced Alison.

Steve exhaled a big rush of air. He already knew what Alison didn't: that DeWaal's Albert Schenk, based on his extensive knowledge of global markets, was going to take over as the new company's director of sales and marketing. Steve was planning to offer Alison a job as head of U.S. marketing, but he wasn't sure she'd take it. He hated the thought of losing her.

"Look, Alison, do me a favor. Try to calm people down a little. I can guarantee you that our best people will have jobs—I'll see to it one way or another. And remember: this deal is going to be rewarding financially to the people who stay—that includes you. So a little more patience is in order. Okay?"

After a pause, Alison quietly responded. "Sure. Okay. Well." She looked a little embarrassed. "Have a good lunch, and watch out for that third martini."

Steve, who rarely drank, forced a smile. With a short wave, Alison left, and Steve realized that his heart was pounding. Four more people about to leave? That was news he could have done without. Just this morning, he had learned that a leading brokerage was downgrading BioHealth's stock from buy to hold. Steve had watched nervously in the past two months as BioHealth's stock price dipped 20% once the initial euphoria over the deal wore off. He knew that part of the drop was attributable to a general softening of the market, but stories about difficulty with the integration process had certainly contributed. As the company's stock options became less valuable to his managers, could he really be so surprised that people were heading for the exits?

Steve picked up the phone and dialed Bruce Bollinger, who would accompany him into the city.

"Bruce, you ready to roll? Let's go."

Going Nowhere Fast

Bruce had been BioHealth's head of HR. It was widely known that Bruce wasn't exactly a workaholic, but in Steve's eyes he made up for his 9-to-5 mentality in other ways. Bruce and Steve went way back. They had worked together for years, and the two played golf together every chance they got. Bruce was known for his stand-up comedy routines at company functions and his good humor on the golf course, which he treated like a second office. More important, he wasn't afraid to give his boss tough messages when he thought Steve needed to hear them, and he had a way of cutting through the baloney at staff meetings. When Kaspar had insisted on naming Christian Meyer as the head of HR, Steve had reluctantly agreed to demote Bruce to director of corporate training.

As Steve walked out of his office, he heard Bruce booming down the hall at him. "Did you see that Tiger pulled out another one? I watched all 18 holes. Unbelievable."

Steve waited for him to catch up and replied, "No, no, I missed it. These days, I'm not sure I'd recognize my clubs if they fell on my big toe."

"You've got to get out more." Bruce continued to analyze Tiger's round until they ducked their heads into the car.

As they drove along, at first rapidly and then haltingly in the stop-and-go traffic of Manhattan, Steve unburdened himself to Bruce about the tough staffing decisions that lay ahead.

"You know, I don't care what the investment bankers say, I like to go with my gut. I like to look people in the eye and find out what they've really got. And I'm not that impressed with a lot of the people from DeWaal. Somehow our guys just seem to get it, and I can't get a good read on the Dutch. All right, so eight of them have left us already. They don't want to move to New York. They're fearful. Alison tells me that our people are too. I mean, I knew the headhunters would be hovering, but I can't believe they got to Sandy Allen. I always thought she would take my job someday, and what really gets me is that I negotiated hard to get the CFO job for her. Anyway, I'm sympathetic to everyone's fears and I'm trying to be as objective as possible, but...Bruce, help me out here."

Bruce looked up from the interview notes and résumés he'd been flipping through. "I think this meeting today is crucial," he said. "We've got to get resolution on our key people. Don't worry, I'll take on Meyer."

Steve hated to admit it, but Christian Meyer had become a bit of a thorn in his side. He wanted to do a lot of testing of the executives—for IQ, for emotional intelligence, for who knew what else. And he constantly talked about the fairness of the process. Steve's view was that fairness was a noble goal—and one they would strive for—but he had to look at the big picture. And speed, as the market was making clear, was crucial.

"We need to get on with this. Even if we don't make the perfect choices right now, we can fix things later. Meanwhile, we've got to consolidate where we can and get the reps up to speed on all our products."

As they pulled up to the restaurant, Bruce got in a final word. "One more thing: if I see Kaspar working his charms on you and getting the upper hand, I'll signal you by knocking over my beer."

Trouble Abroad

They had reserved a small private room at the restaurant. Steve and Bruce were on time; Kaspar and Christian, staying at a nearby hotel, walked in 15 minutes later. After an exchange of pleasantries, the four sat down and ordered.

Steve, remembering what he'd been told about European corporate etiquette, held back from jumping straight to business. He reminded himself that they had the rest of the afternoon. Still, unlike his counterpart, he wasn't much for small talk—and Kaspar's discourse ran from the fate of the euro to Quentin Tarantino, from Afro-Cuban music to the problems of reaching the world's poorest people with desperately needed medications.

That last topic, in a roundabout way, finally got them to the task at hand as the coffee arrived. Both DeWaal and BioHealth had several foreign plants, and Steve wanted to nail down which ones would remain open and who would run them.

Steve's plan for Asia went like this: they would close the DeWaal plant in Indonesia, which was redundant, and keep the BioHealth plant in Shanghai. Steve believed it was imperative to maintain a presence in China, and he was prepared to offer someone from DeWaal the number two spot there to sweeten the pill.

Meanwhile, the Dutch company had an operation in Bangalore, India, and the U.S. company had one in Bombay. The Bangalore plant was extremely efficient, and Steve was prepared—in the interests of fairness and despite his fear of seeing the headline "Lindell Caves to van de Velde (Again)"—to close down the Bombay operation. The question was who to put in charge. The Dutch fellow—what was his name, Peter Krug?—had headed up the Bangalore operations for three years, and his résumé was impressive. But Steve had a candidate too. Vijay Naipaul, who had been in the United States the past ten years since coming to business school from Delhi, was an ambitious and talented executive. If not for the merger, Steve would have put him in charge of operations at the Bombay plant. Being in charge of India would be his dream job, and Steve had been told by his COO that Vijay might walk if he didn't get the job. Steve hoped that Kaspar wasn't too attached to Krug.

He quickly laid out his thoughts on Asia, hoping to move on to the touchy question of R&D management.

Kaspar looked up from his espresso and broke into a broad grin. "Oh dear, Steve, what are you saying. You know they will have my head in Rotterdam if we close the Indonesia plant—ties to the former colonies and all that. And you know, there are outstanding people running that plant. Really and truly! As for India, well, yes, by all means close the plant, but can we decide so quickly who will run the remaining one? Christian tells me we have a ways to go in the process of deciding such matters—isn't that so, Christian?"

Steve jumped in. "Well, I'm sure we could find another spot for Krug. Perhaps if he and Naipaul were coleaders of the Bombay plant...."

He was interrupted by the sound of a beer bottle falling to the floor.

How should Steve decide who stays and who goes?

Four commentators offer their advice.

> **DAVID KIDD** *is a partner at Egon Zehnder International in Chicago, where he leads the firm's global management appraisal process.*

Many mergers do not create the shareholder value expected of them. The combination of cultural differences and an ill-conceived human resource integration strategy is one of the most common reasons for that failure. Given the well-publicized war for talent, I am constantly surprised by how little attention is paid to the matter of human capital during mergers.

Steve Lindell must be single-minded in staffing the new organization with outstanding people. For all his emphasis on speed, he has moved too slowly. At the same time, he is unwise to think he can make selection decisions now and fix them later if they don't work out. In light of today's competition for world-class executives, this is extremely shortsighted. It is irresponsible to allow talented individuals to leave, and it is time consuming, risky, and expensive to replace them later.

Steve seems to have shown up for the lunch meeting without an overall plan for HR integration. It's not surprising, then, that he's prepared to make decisions haphazardly. He should have come to the table with a plan that, at the very least, included a strategy to retain key executives (possibly by paying them a bonus when the merger is completed), a communication plan to ease their fears, an evaluation and selection process for the top levels in the new organization, and a process to harmonize the two companies' contractual terms and compensation plans—which are often quite different in the United States from those in Europe.

Although off to a bad start, the lunch meeting is still salvageable. Steve and Kaspar must get to work and put together an overall plan. Once the two leaders have agreed to a plan, Steve should embark on a formal effort to evaluate all the top executives of the two companies. An appraisal process would be helpful to Steve for several reasons:

- **Executive Competencies.** It's not clear that anyone has considered the competencies that DeWaal Bio-Health will require from its leadership group to deliver superior performance. The first step in the process should be to define these competencies and their associated behavioral indicators.

- **Objectivity.** Steve admits to Bruce that he is not very impressed with the Dutch executives. This is a common problem in any merger, where the tendency is to favor the people you know. It's important to evaluate the executives in a way that is transparent to both sides; the key is to take the bias and emotion out of the selection process and ensure that the most qualified people are chosen.

- **Fairness.** Christian isn't the only one concerned about fairness; the Americans are also worried about who has the power and how that's going to affect them. Using an objective appraisal process lets executives know that the deck is not stacked against them. It gives them ample opportunity to present their credentials and demonstrate how they match the competencies that the new company requires.

- **Benchmarking.** Unless the merged companies are absolutely committed to appointing everyone from within, the appraisal process should measure all executives against their peers outside the company.

The best approach, in my experience, is to bring in outside help to perform the appraisal. External consultants can provide valuable expertise to the HR integration process, conducting in-depth, structured interviews and collecting 360-degree feedback. As objective participants in the process, these outsiders view the situation without the baggage of internal politics, loyalties, and cultural or power clashes. They are more likely to make accurate assessments of how the candidate pool of executives matches the required competencies. They also tend to be more creative in identifying other roles within the company for those people who are real assets but who came in second during the competition for slots. And outsiders offer a much-needed benchmarking perspective, pointing out when the company might need to go outside to fill a newly defined role.

The sad truth is that Steve could have avoided losing valuable employees by focusing on the problem sooner. Imagine how much better off he would be if he had conducted the evaluation of top executives as part of the due-diligence process, as some forward-thinking companies are doing today.

Steve, unfortunately, is learning the hard way about the challenges of integration. But if he adopts this approach, he has every chance of retaining his key executives and assembling a great team. This will serve him well on the road to a successful merger.

LAWRENCE J. DEMONACO *is senior vice president of human resources at GE Capital in Stamford, Connecticut.*

Steve has brought a softball to a hardball game. He's forgotten that the success of any merger or acquisition starts with an understanding of power—who has it and how you use it. Now Steve needs to push harder on Kaspar to move the integration along. He's had enough experience with the DeWaal leader to recognize that Kaspar's behavior at the lunch is Kaspar's character—period. If Steve continues to try to "understand" Kaspar, he'll become even more tentative. He has to say to his counterpart, "We've done enough noodling. It's time to make decisions." Because making a decision—even one that leads you to say later, "I wish I hadn't done that"—is better than doing nothing at all.

In the integration process, speed is critical. A few years ago, I talked with 25 CEOs of companies that we had acquired and asked them to identify the one thing we should have done differently in the process. All but one said that we hadn't gone fast enough with the integration.

What Steve needs to do immediately is bring together the top people they have already chosen and make them into the nucleus of a selection team. I'm not sure, however, if either guy from HR should be involved. They both have serious limitations. Christian can't make decisions himself; he wants test results or a computer to do the job for him. Bruce, on the other hand, has some good instincts, and he's not afraid to push back and tell Steve what he really thinks. But he acts like a clown.

So before the selection team meets, Steve and Kaspar should pull Christian aside and say, "Look, we're here to decide today. We don't have the time for testing or for any touchy-feely things. If you're going to continue down that path, you'll become an obstructionist, and we don't want you at the meeting." And if Steve wants Bruce to participate in the meeting, he has to have a similarly tough conversation and say, basically, "Quit being a clown. I want your help, but you've got to act like a grown-up."

At the meeting, Steve should present the criteria for selection—the emphasis should be on business success, decisiveness, and communication and relationship skills. A merger is not a good time to pick the people who need an extra week to get things done or who prefer to have their lunch slipped to them under the office door. The team should debate the criteria and then select as many top people as possible. It should be stipulated that no one leaves the room until they've made their decisions— including backup choices for people who turn them down, and alternative jobs for people they have to exclude from the top 65 but still want to keep. Then they should notify people and give them a day to decide if they want to stay.

One thing that Steve seems to have forgotten to do is reassure people who are vital to the success of the company, like Alison, that they are needed and important. The selection team should go to these people and speak plainly. "Here are our projections for one, three, five years out. If we overlay your options on these figures, this is a big nut. And let me talk to you about opportunity.

There are going to be opportunities you've never dreamed of." In fact, I'd go after Sandy Allen and use every trick in the book to get her back. Steve should tell her, "I need you more now than ever. I want you to replace me someday." Imagine the boost it would give morale if one of the defectors came back to the company and said, "I made a mistake."

Finally, Steve needs a plan for himself. If Kaspar can't "hear" Steve's message about the need for speed and continues to stiff-arm him, what should Steve do? By accepting that treatment, he's making decisions about who's in charge. So before he sits down with the selection team, he has to decide at what point it would be best to walk away from the table. If things get to that point, he has to be prepared to move on.

GRANT FREELAND *is a vice president at the Boston Consulting Group in Boston.*

Both Steve and Kaspar may think they are focused on selecting key people and that their approach is best. But they are wrong on at least three counts.

First, Steve and Kaspar are at odds about the importance of speed in selecting the new company's top management. Kaspar seems unconcerned about the slow pace, and Steve is right to feel a sense of urgency. Stabilizing the senior team is a critical short-term task and needs to happen as quickly as possible. But it's not enough simply to "get on with this" because we can always "fix things later." The senior executives who are selected will drive the success or failure of the new organization. Poor decisions will have a long-term impact.

Second, it's not clear that Kaspar and Steve are actually using facts to help them make decisions. It's foolish, for example, to design a plant network haphazardly over lunch when they could be using in-depth analyses of cost, quality, and service to make objective decisions. They should be using such data to get the best answer and, equally important, to signal to staff that decisions are not being made arbitrarily.

Third, neither of the two leaders has shown that he can rise above cultural differences. Steve says that his people "just seem to get it," and Kaspar wants to protect his staff in Indonesia. When senior managers look at their future colleagues exclusively through the lens of their own culture, it's no surprise that selection problems arise. The underlying attitude is that "they" are not like "us," and therefore they are no good. Kaspar and Steve must learn to separate a candidate's style—which may reflect corporate culture—from his or her potential performance in the new organization.

Given these problems, what should the selection process be? Christian Meyer is right to be concerned about fairness, but his approach sounds more like a compilation of the latest HR fads than a process shaped by an understanding of the business needs facing the new company.

Fairness is achieved by having a well-planned and broadly communicated process. Senior management must communicate clearly and frequently the details of the process, including timing and selection criteria. When people don't have such information, they tend to assume the worst, as Alison's comments make clear.

Kaspar and Steve have to make explicit the business objectives of their selection process. For example, will candidates for key jobs be selected purely on the basis of individual performance? Is there a rationale for keeping more of one company's leaders in areas of particular geographical or functional strengths? Is the goal to achieve a merger of equals by balancing the senior executive teams with a 50-50 split of positions? Or will one company merit a greater number of executives because of its larger size or deeper experience? When two people are equally valued, what are the tiebreaking criteria?

Whatever the specific goals are, selection should be done in waves: the first level appointed should help select the second level, and so on. The process should be rigorous but not cumbersome. We would expect the company to interview multiple candidates for each senior-management position, to evaluate past perfor- mance reviews, and even to solicit evaluations from third parties such as executive recruiting firms. Some very tal- ented people may not fit an immediate opening, and they should be managed and retained in a systematic way. Finally, it's useful to informally assure the stars of each company that they will have a place in the new organiza- tion—but you should make such promises only if they can be kept. At the end of the day, there will always be some horse trading. But horse trading ought to come at the end of the integration process, not at the beginning, and it should be the exception, not the rule.

As they finish their lunch, Steve and Kaspar seem well on their way to creating one of the many mergers that destroy shareholder value. They need to put down their drinks, stop worrying about who is perceived to have more power, and develop a selection approach that will ensure that the new company's top slots are filled with the best executive for each position.

PATRICK O'SULLIVAN *is the CEO of Zurich Financial Services Property and Casualty Insurance and Banking Divisions in the United Kingdom, Ireland, and South Africa.*

Instead of acting like the CEO of a major company,

Steve is trying to make it all happen himself. His first mistake was to focus on getting regulatory approval while letting everything else languish for two months. He should have appointed a team of lawyers to deal with that issue, providing direction only as needed.

At the same time, Steve hasn't done a good job communicating with his people or building the executive team, as his conversation with Alison makes clear. He needs to move quickly to keep his top talent. If there are a few people that he wants to keep, he has to talk to them before they walk out the door. He should tell them, "I can't guarantee anything, but I want you in this organization. Pick up the phone anytime you're bothered, but don't look for another job. And come see me if you're offered one."

If there are too many people for Steve to talk to personally, he should make sure that someone else who has already been picked for the new company is talking to them. Another way to retain key managers is by using what we call "stay pay," which is a bonus for people who stay until after the merger is approved.

Steve needs to get the top team in place and working together as quickly as possible. Steve should have started the process by meeting with each of the three people he had chosen for his team so far, and then with Kaspar and his three similarly chosen people. As soon as he and Kaspar decide on direct reports, Steve needs to get this team working together on delivering the key results of the merger. Steve's major priority has to be to deliver the benefits of the merger that were promised to shareholders and the public.

In addition, Steve needs to take the lead in forging a relationship with Kaspar. Though it may not be easy, these two need to work through important cultural and organizational differences and come to a meeting of the minds very soon. If they end up competing during the early stages of the merger, the rest of the organization may follow suit, with predictable results.

I went through a process like this not long ago. I was CEO of Eagle Star Insurance when the press broke the news in October 1997 that the company was merging with the Zurich Group. We locked the deal and got shareholder approval in December, and then we had to wait nine months to get regulatory approval.

I was confirmed as CEO of the merged company in January and then was given one month to choose my new management team. During that month, I interviewed all the people I didn't know, and then made my recommendations to the Zurich Group's chairman and CEO. My direct reports then had to push on with the task of selecting their teams, a total of about 250 people from a pool of 400. The long wait for regulatory approval made this part of the process difficult. We did everything we could to reassure people and to get them to stay while we made our selections and formed the merged company.

This process was all the more difficult since the company had to make a major turnaround in financial performance in the midst of this merger. The urgency of our situation forced us to focus on something that is crucial to the success of any merger—bringing people together as quickly as possible to find effective ways to run the organization better. This applied to the top team as well. In the process, we rapidly built one new company, one that is thriving today.

Steve needs to drive this merger with the same intensity he would if the company were failing. By concentrating his efforts on crucial elements of the merger—getting the top team in place quickly, building an effective relationship with Kaspar, and focusing the organization on achieving performance goals—he is much more likely to make this merger a success.

Originally published in January 2001

Making the Deal Real

How GE Capital
Integrates Acquisitions

RONALD N. ASHKENAS,

LAWRENCE J. DEMONACO,

AND SUZANNE C. FRANCIS

Executive Summary

MOST COMPANIES view acquisitions and mergers as onetime events managed with heroic effort—anxiety-producing experiences that often result in lost jobs, restructured responsibilities, derailed careers, and diminished power. Little wonder, then, that most managers think about how to get them over with—not how to do them better. But even as the number of mergers and acquisitions rises in the United States, studies show the performance of the resulting companies falls below industry averages more often than not.

To improve these statistics, executives need to view acquisition integration as a manageable process, not a unique event. One company that has done exactly that is GE Capital Services, which has assimilated more than 100 acquisitions in the past five years alone and, in the process, has developed a formal model for melding new acquisitions into the corporate fold.

Drawing on their experiences working with the company to develop the model, consultants Ron Ashkenas and Suzanne Francis, together with GE Capital's Lawrence DeMonaco, offer four lessons from the company's successful run. First, begin the integration process before the deal is signed. Second, dedicate a full-time individual to managing the integration process. Third, implement any necessary restructuring sooner rather than later. And fourth, integrate not only the business operations but also the corporate cultures. These guidelines won't erase all of the discomfort that accompanies many mergers, but they can make the process more transparent and predictable for those involved.

LIKE THE PROCESS by which a child learns to walk, most business innovations emerge from dozens of trial-and-error experiments; from seemingly random actions that eventually form a pattern; from hundreds of small, almost imperceptible adjustments that eventually result in a solid step forward. This has been true for developments ranging from lean manufacturing to concurrent product development to business process reengineering—all now well-accepted innovations that emerged from dozens of experiments until they crystallized to form a methodology others could follow.

An exception to this rule thus far has been innovation relating to acquisition integration—the process by which one company melds with another after the deal is done. Most acquisitions and mergers are onetime events that companies manage with heroic effort; few companies go through the process often enough to develop a pattern. Thus it tends to be seen not as a process—as something replicable—but only as something to get finished, so everyone can get back to business.

The tendency to see integration as a unique event in an organization's life is magnified by the fact that acquisitions and mergers often are painful and anxiety-producing experiences. *No wonder most managers think about how to get acquisitions over with—not how to do them better.* They involve job loss, restructured responsibilities, derailed careers, diminished power, and much else that is stressful. No wonder most managers think about how to get them over with—not how to do them better the next time.

Improving the acquisition integration process, however, may be one of the most urgent and compelling challenges facing businesses today. Industry consolidations, the globalization of competition, technological developments, and other trends have touched off an unprecedented wave of mergers and acquisitions that shows no signs of abating. According to figures from the Securities Data Company published in the *New York Times*, the dollar value of U.S. mergers and acquisitions announced in 1996 alone grew more than 27% to $658.8 billion from $518 billion in 1995.

Despite this enormous growth in merger activity, acquisitions that appear to be both financially and strategically sound on paper often turn out to be disappointing for many companies: the acquiring company takes too many years to realize the expected synergies or is unable to get people to work together productively or puts the companies together in such a heavy-handed way that the unique capabilities of the acquired company (its

best people and most valued customers, for example)
melt away. Perhaps that's why a study reported last January in the *Economist* of 300 major mergers conducted
over a ten-year period by Mercer Management Consulting found that in 57% of these merged companies return
to shareholders lagged behind the average for their
industries.

Given this confluence of events—a growing number
of mergers and acquisitions combined with high failure
rates—it is increasingly important that executives learn
how to manage the integration of acquisitions as a replicable process and not as a onetime-only event. One
company to learn from is GE Capital Services—an organization that has made more than 100 acquisitions in the
past five years, resulting in a 30% increase in its workforce, the rapid globalization of its businesses, and a doubling of its net income. GE Capital has been working to
make acquisition integration a core capability and a
competitive advantage that will enable it to continue its
growth in the future.

For the past three years, we have been part of a team
that has helped GE Capital learn from its extensive
acquisition-integration experience to create a more
replicable process. We have interviewed dozens of managers and staff members from both acquiring and
acquired businesses, including many who after being
acquired by GE Capital became acquirers themselves.
Using these interviews and related documents and materials, we have helped GE Capital create a model for
acquisition integration. This model has been fine-tuned
through workshops with GE Capital's many acquisition-integration experts, and it has been applied successfully
to several recent integration efforts. (See the exhibit
"The Wheel of Fortune.")

Growth Through Acquisition

To appreciate the lessons GE Capital has learned about acquisition integration, it is important to understand that GE Capital itself is the product of dozens of acquisitions that have been blended to form one of the world's largest financial-services organizations.

GE Capital was founded in 1933 as a subsidiary of the General Electric Company to provide consumers with credit to purchase GE appliances. Since then, the company has grown to become a major financial-services conglomerate with 27 separate businesses, more than 50,000 employees worldwide (nearly half of them outside the United States), and a net income in 1996 of $2.8 billion. The businesses that generate these returns range from private-label credit-card services to commercial real-estate financing to railcar and aircraft leasing. More than half of these businesses became part of GE Capital through acquisitions.

For the past decade, since Gary Wendt became chairman of GE Capital, the company's plans for growth have included acquiring companies. Thus every business is constantly seeking acquisitions. To engineer these deals, each executive vice president (who heads a group of businesses) has a Business Development, or BD, officer. Larger businesses within each group have their own BD officer, and Wendt also has BD people on his staff. Those professionals, many from consulting firms, focus on finding, analyzing, and negotiating acquisitions that will contribute to GE Capital's growth.

The acquisitions come in different shapes and sizes. Sometimes, the acquisition is a portfolio or asset purchase that adds volume to a particular business without adding people. Sometimes, it is a consolidating acquisition in which a company is purchased and then

The Wheel of Fortune

Over the years, GE Capital Services' acquisition-integration process has been discussed, debated, tested, changed, and refined. It is now established well enough to be codified in what we call the Pathfinder Model.

The model divides the process into four "action stages," starting with the work that goes on before the acquisition is completed—that is, before the deal closes—and continuing all the way through assimilation. There are two or three subprocesses in each action stage, such as due diligence during the preacquisition stage and strategy formulation during the foundation-building stage. Finally, each action stage includes several best practices—specific and practical steps managers can take to support the process.

The model's neat and systematic appearance belies the fact that acquisition integration is as much art as science. The Pathfinder Model recommends a particular sequence of leveraged actions, but there are aspects of every acquisition-integration process that are new or unique. As in any major organizational transformation, managers will have to improvise. The model, however, can prevent improvisation from becoming the whole show.

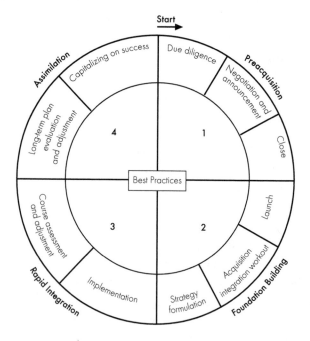

The Wheel of Fortune (continued)

1. **Preacquisition**
   - Begin cultural assessment
   - Identify business/cultural barriers to integration success
   - Select integration manager
   - Assess strengths/weaknesses of business and function leaders
   - Develop communication strategy

2. **Foundation Building**
   - Formally introduce integration manager
   - Orient new executives to GE Capital business rhythms and nonnegotiables
   - Jointly formulate integration plan, including 100-day and communication plans
   - Visibly involve senior management
   - Provide sufficient resources and assign accountability

3. **Rapid Integration**
   - Use process mapping, CAP, and workout to accelerate integration
   - Use audit staff for process audits
   - Use feedback and learning to continually adapt integration plan
   - Initiate short-term management exchange

4. **Assimilation**
   - Continue developing common tools, practices, processes, and language
   - Continue longer-term management exchanges
   - Utilize corporate education center and Crotonville
   - Use audit staff for integration audit

consolidated into an existing GE Capital business. That happened when GE Capital Vendor Financial Services bought Chase Manhattan Bank's leasing business. Sometimes, the acquisition moves into fresh territory, spawning an entirely new GE Capital business. GE Capital made such a "platform," or strategic, acquisition when it bought the Travelers Corporation's Mortgage Services business. And finally, sometimes, the acquisition is a hybrid, parts of which fit into one or more existing businesses while other parts stand alone or become joint ventures.

From these acquisitions, and its efforts to make them work on a financial and organizational basis, GE Capital has learned the following four lessons:

LESSON 1

Acquisition integration is not a discrete phase of a deal and does not begin when the documents are signed. Rather, it is a process that begins with due diligence and runs through the ongoing management of the new enterprise. Any manager who has been involved with an acquisition will agree that the process proceeds through a number of fairly predictable stages: selecting possible acquisitions, narrowing the field, agreeing on a first-choice candidate, assessing compliance with regulations, convening preliminary discussions, formulating a letter of intent, conducting due diligence, completing financial negotiations, making the announcement, signing the agreement, and closing the deal. And given these stages, it is natural to assume that integration would begin after the deal is closed.

For many years, GE Capital, like most organizations, proceeded under that assumption. Business development specialists, working with business leaders and finance experts, saw most of the deals through to closing. After the documents were signed and the mementos exchanged, managers were expected to take over and begin the integration process.

The realization that integration is not a stage following the deal came about through experience.

Unfortunately, in most cases, that approach to integration was less than effective. Integration was slow and costly. There were constant surprises about peoples' reactions to being acquired, and financial returns were often hindered by delays in putting the companies together. In some cases, when acquisitions did succeed, it was mainly because the acquired company was left alone and not integrated into GE Capital.

Necessity mothers invention. Like most things an organization learns, the realization that integration is not a stage following the deal, and could be done faster and more effectively if it were begun sooner, came about through experience. In the mid-1980s, GE Capital acquired Dart & Kraft Leasing and Kerr Leasing, intending to integrate Kerr into D&K. In the midst of that integration process, GE Capital acquired Gelco Corporation, a much larger leasing company that also included other financial-services businesses. At that point, the acquisition strategy called for integrating both D&K and Kerr into Gelco's auto-fleet-leasing business, spinning off some other pieces of Gelco into freestanding businesses, and selling some nonstrategic pieces of the company.

In short, this was no simple acquisition integration, and many of GE Capital's senior executives were concerned that the standard approaches to integration would be inadequate.

As a response, a human resources executive suggested that the company's communication expert use the regulatory review period before the Gelco acquisition closed to create a comprehensive communication plan for the forthcoming integration. But instead of just a communication plan, what emerged was the framework for an entire integration strategy. That strategy included a 48-hour communication blitz directed at employees immediately after the deal closed; the formulation of a role in the new organization for the former Gelco, D&K, and Kerr executives; a strategy for presenting the acquisition to the media; a way to handle some necessary consolidations of headquarters staff; and an outplacement plan.

Most important, the framework signaled a new way of thinking about integration—a recognition that there were predictable issues that could be anticipated long before the deal actually closed. The Gelco acquisition turned out to be a watershed for GE Capital, a demonstration that extremely complex transactions could be assimilated more successfully by planning for integration well before the closing.

Integrating: earlier is better. Eventually, the planning process began to extend back even further—into the due diligence phase—as GE Capital executives realized that thinking about integration that early could speed the eventual melding. In the early 1990s, that thinking was formalized during due diligence for a Chicago-based equipment-leasing company. The head of the due diligence effort, having seen how effective the Gelco plan had been, convened a series of end-of-day meetings for the functional captains of the various due-diligence teams (including finance, operations, systems, human resources, and sales) to discuss what they had learned each day and to develop preliminary plans for managing the acquisition after the deal closed.

Applying those lessons to subsequent acquisitions, GE Capital found that being sensitive to integration issues during the due diligence phase began to foster better decisions about whether to proceed with an acquisition at all. During the final stages of due diligence for the acquisition of a British leasing-equipment company, for example, two senior business leaders from GE Capital had a working lunch with the CEO and CFO of the company, expressly to discuss some of GE Capital's expectations for how the merged company would be run. During lunch, significant differences in basic management styles and values became clear. The conversation led GE Capital to take a harder look at the management culture of the target company and to realize that integration could be difficult and contentious. On that basis, despite very favorable financials, GE Capital walked away from the transaction.

Recognizing that planning for integration can begin with the very first discussions gave GE Capital a head start.

Today recognizing that planning for integration can begin with the very first discussions gives GE Capital a head start in bringing new companies into the fold. For example, during investigations relating to the credit card business of a major European retailer, the due diligence team learned that employees of the soon-to-be-acquired company were concerned that they might lose their traditional shopping-discount benefit at the retailer's stores. GE Capital persuaded the retailer to continue the discount for one year after the acquisition and also agreed to make up the difference of the lost benefit in subsequent years by adding approximately $200 to each employee's paycheck. As a result, GE Capital turned a potential cause of friction into a positive experience that led to boosted morale (as measured through attitude surveys), greater receptivity to other changes, and higher productivity.

LESSON 2

Integration management is a full-time job and needs to be recognized as a distinct business function, just like operations, marketing, or finance. Since acquisition integration is an ongoing process and not a discrete stage of a deal, someone needs to manage it. That may seem obvious, but in reality the issue is complex—one that GE Capital has grappled with for more than a decade.

Let's look at the key players in an acquisition: The acquiring business usually will have a due diligence team that includes people from such areas as finance, tax, business development, human resources, and technology. It will have a "leader" (GE's term for a general manager) who is the ultimate "buyer" of the company. Similarly, the acquired business will have a business leader and a full complement of managers and staff.

Who among that cast of characters focuses on integration? Who is the one person responsible for making sure that the new company becomes a fully functioning, high-performing part of the acquirer?

For many years at GE Capital, the answer to that question was unclear. The due diligence team, which developed the deepest knowledge of the new company and had the best insight into what would be needed to integrate it after the deal closed, usually disbanded after the deal was struck, its members returning to their regular jobs or moving on to the next transaction. The functional and business leaders of the acquiring GE company typically focused only on the integration of their particular units.

The newly acquired business leaders, who had the most incentive to integrate and learn how to be successful with their new owners, did not have sufficient knowledge of GE Capital, its resources, or its integration requirements. What's more, they tended to be preoccupied with running the company and also with a host of personal issues—protecting, reassuring, or outplacing their people; figuring out whether they wanted to stay in the new company; and (perhaps unconsciously) proving that their company was even better than the buyers thought.

Given those realities, the business leader of the acquiring GE business was usually assumed to be accountable for integration. But for a number of reasons, that was an unrealistic assignment. In most cases, the business leader had other units to run and was not dedicated fully to the new acquisition. And even when the business leader was able to devote time to the acquisition, his or her focus usually was not on integrating the cultures, processes, and people but, appropriately, on such critical business issues as profit growth, staffing key jobs, and customer retention.

Furthermore, the business leader's very position of authority often limited his or her ability to facilitate integration. People in a newly acquired company need someone they can talk to freely, to ask "stupid" questions, find out how things work at GE Capital, and discover what resources are available and how to use them. They need a guide to the new culture and a bridge between their company and GE Capital. The last person who fits that role is the new boss they want to impress.

A role is born. At GE Capital, the role of designated integration manager evolved, as most innovations do, through a combination of chance and necessity. Consider, again, the case of Gelco. At the time, it was GE Capital's largest acquisition. Larry Toole, a senior human-resources executive who had been involved in the due diligence effort, was asked to stay on and support the newly acquired Gelco team. Toole (now GE Capital's head of human resources) acted as a facilitator to the new leadership team. He brought groups of people from GE Capital and Gelco together in work sessions to develop common plans; he oriented the new team to GE Capital's requirements; he made sure that the soft sides of the integration (such as communication and benefits) were taken into account; and he counseled Gelco's senior managers about how to succeed in GE Capital.

By the end of the 1980s, it was clear that the Gelco integration had gone well. But the critical role that Toole had played as an integration manager was not fully recognized until several other acquisitions that had no integration managers failed to proceed as smoothly. For example, no integration manager was assigned when GE Capital's retail credit-card business bought the credit card operations of the Burton Group (a U.K. retailer) in 1991. Two years later, when the unit was not meeting expectations, a reintegration effort, which did include a full-time integration manager, turned the situation around.

By 1994, it was apparent that the integration manager was a key role. Then the questions became, Who would

make a good integration manager? and How should the
job actually work?

An accidental role becomes an intentional strategy.
Today two types of people are generally selected to be
integration managers in GE Capital—the *high-potential*
individual and the *experienced hand.* The high-potential
manager is usually a less seasoned person with strong
functional credentials who is viewed as a future business
leader. That type of person is widely employed in small,
straightforward, or highly structured integration efforts.
For more complex acquisitions or those that incorporate
multiple businesses, an experienced hand—someone
who knows GE Capital well and has proven management
skills—usually takes on the integration job.

In all cases, the integration managers that have been
most effective have been those that have served on the
due diligence team. The integration manager then becomes a full-fledged member of the leadership team for
the acquired business, reporting directly to its business
leader. Selection of the integration manager is based as
much on personal characteristics as on technical skills. In
the past several years, the backgrounds of successful integration managers have been drawn from fields as diverse
as human resources, auditing, finance, technology, marketing, and law. Some need to be skilled in a second language. But all have strong interpersonal skills and are
sensitive to cultural differences. All have the ability to
facilitate groups and a deep knowledge of how GE Capital
works. And all have the energy to do what it takes to
make an integration successful. (See "What It Takes to Be
an Integration Manager," at the end of this article.)

Given the job's broad range of responsibilities, it
would seem natural to hold the integration manager

accountable for the performance of the business. But GE Capital's experience suggests that doing so reduces the accountability of both the business leader and the rest of the leadership team. And in reality, the integration manager does not control the critical business resources. Instead of having P&L responsibility then, most of GE Capital's integration managers are held accountable for the creation and delivery of a disciplined integration plan and for reaching the plan's milestones. In reaching those milestones, the integration manager acts more as a consultant than anything else. The job is to build connective tissue between GE Capital and the new organization, tissue that will allow information and resources to pass freely back and forth, tissue that will become self-generating over time.

An example from a European acquisition illustrates how the integration manager builds connective tissue. After completing the acquisition, the business leader asked the integration manager to quickly introduce the new company to GE's integrity policy. At GE, integrity is not just embodied in a standard corporate-policy statement. It is a detailed requirement meant to ensure that every employee understands what constitutes proper and improper ways of conducting business.

Given the importance of the integrity policy, the business leader expected that the material would be immediately reprinted, distributed, and used in dozens of meetings mandatory for all employees. But the integration manager took another tack. He asked a few senior managers from the new company how people would react to GE's policy. The response was a surprise: "If we send that out, it will be like saying to our people that before GE came along we didn't have any integrity!"

To avoid such a reaction, the integration manager quickly commissioned a small group of managers and staff members to develop a constructive way to convey the integrity policy. The group decided that its own managers (rather than GE's people) should introduce the policy at a series of all-employee meetings. They introduced those meetings by saying, "One of the benefits of belonging to GE is that they have made explicit the principles of integrity that we have always followed in our company but that we never had the resources to write down. And here they are . . ."

That may seem like a small matter, but the accumulation of such small matters can destroy the connective tissue between companies. The job of the integration manager is to keep that tissue growing.

LESSON 3

Decisions about management structure, key roles, reporting relationships, layoffs, restructuring, and other career-affecting aspects of the integration should be made, announced, and implemented as soon as possible after the deal is signed—within days, if possible. Creeping changes, uncertainty, and anxiety that last for months are debilitating and immediately start to drain value from an acquisition. With all the tension of a medieval passion play, at the moment that an acquisition closes, an intense drama begins to unfold between the new owners and their new employees. On one side of the stage are the acquirer's managers, who almost always believe they can run the acquired company better—whether through the introduction of new capital, new technology, new resources, new energy, or new ideas. And since acquisitions come at a price, one aspect of their agenda almost always is to reduce costs.

Playing opposite the new managers are all the employees of the acquired company—from senior management to shipping-dock staff. Their script tells them that when companies are purchased, the acquiring company often puts its own people in charge, changes policies and procedures, restructures, consolidates, and generally takes over. So they walk onto the stage of the new company feeling anxious, insecure, uncertain, and even angry. Who are these new owners? What are their intentions? Can we trust what they say? Do we still have jobs, and are they the same as before? Why did our previous owners sell? Did we do a bad job, or did they betray us?

In short, the acquiring managers close the deal with a certain amount of euphoria, ready to get on with the exciting challenge of running the new business better. But the staff members needed to keep things running and make improvements are preoccupied with issues of security and identity. They have no interest in a close-the-deal party; they just want to know if they still have jobs.

If left unrecognized, this psychodrama can be debilitating and can send the integration process down the wrong path. On one hand, when issues of security are not addressed immediately, levels of productivity, customer service, and innovation quickly deteriorate as employees focus on their own needs rather than on those of the company. On the other hand, if acquiring managers restructure quickly but without sensitivity, they risk beginning their tenure without the trust and respect of the remaining staff. The challenge is to avoid both traps, to make structural changes as quickly as possible but in a way that maintains everyone's dignity. If that challenge is not met, successful integration may not be possible.

First things first: Do I have a job?　Most acquisitions involve restructuring, either to improve the efficiency of the acquired unit or to ensure that its organization fits with that of the new owner. But moving quickly to restructure is not easy, even when obvious changes need to be made. Often the new owners fear that early layoffs will send the signal that they are the "bad guys." So they delay the inevitable until the "right" time. Or the new owners may worry about the publicity and the potential impact on their company's image—so they, too, wait to make layoffs, imagining that they can be made quietly later, when no one is watching. And in some situations, the new owners worry that they do not have enough experience with the company and its staff, that they will make mistakes. So they want to wait until they get to know everyone and understand the company better.

For many years, GE Capital struggled both with the challenge of finding the right time to restructure acquisitions and with the decision of when, or if, to bring in new managers. Sometimes, structural moves were delayed for many months after the company had been bought. The realization that this was a mistake came in 1991, one year after the acquisition of a finance company in Europe. It was obvious when the company was purchased that restructuring was needed. Twelve layers of management (which worked out to one manager for every two employees) had created a high-cost, high-control organization whose ability to innovate and change was highly limited. Yet despite the obvious need for "de-layering" and cost reduction, GE Capital kept all the members of the management team in place and allowed them to keep the organization intact. That was done for a number of seemingly rational reasons: fear of destroying morale, lack of confidence about which managers to let go, and a feeling that here was a European culture that GE Capital perhaps did not fully understand.

A year passed. Costs remained high, and performance remained low. Finally, GE Capital's business leader stepped in and forced a thorough consolidation. The surprise was the staff's reaction. Instead of being upset, most employees (as reported in surveys) wondered why GE Capital had taken so long. They had seen the need for cost reduction from the beginning and had spent much of the year waiting for the plans to be announced.

We have interviewed ten CEOs of companies that GE Capital has acquired from different countries about the pace of consolidation. All have said the same thing: "Although at the time we thought that things were moving too quickly, in retrospect, you did not go fast enough." In short, they said that there is no such thing as an acquisition that does not include some degree of change—in either structure, philosophy, systems, or strategy. Their message was this: if change is inevitable, let's get on with it rather than allow anxiety and speculation to diffuse energy and focus.

Restructure with respect. A crucial springboard to successful integration is the manner in which restructuring is carried out. First and foremost, the acquiring company needs to be straightforward about what is happening and what is planned. Even when the news is bad, the one thing the staff of newly acquired companies appreciates most is the truth. That includes being able to say "we don't know" about certain areas or "we have not yet decided" about others. It also includes sharing information about when and by what process a decision may be reached. The truth also means acknowledging some of the stress and other emotions. As one CEO of an acquired company wisely noted, "Never tell the acquired staff that it will be 'business as usual' when it will never be the same for them again. And don't tell them that this was a 'merger of equals' when you have clearly taken them over. And don't tell them that they have 'a wonderful future' to look forward to when they are still confused and grieving over the past."

Never tell the acquired staff that it will be "business as usual" when it never will be again.

Second, it is critical to treat those individuals who will be negatively affected with dignity, respect, and support. Not only is this the right thing to do, it is also a powerful way to show those who remain what kind of company they now are working for—and to help them develop positive feelings.

But the most powerful way to move ahead is to get the employees of the acquired company focused on the real work of growing the newly formed business. How to shift the focus toward the future, and get people to start working on it, is the last lesson from GE Capital's experience.

LESSON 4

A successful integration melds not only the various technical aspects of the businesses but also the different cultures. The best way to do so is to get people working together quickly to solve business problems and accomplish results that could not have been achieved before. In many ways, an acquisition is like an arranged marriage: the "parents" negotiate the deal, sign the contract, and then expect the "newlyweds" to live together in harmony. An arranged marriage, however, has a much better chance of success than an acquisition does since only one couple is involved, and the parties usually come from similar cultures and share common values. In acquisitions, many people—sometimes thousands—need to learn how to live together, and the values and mind-sets of the acquiring and acquired organizations almost always differ. That disparity is even more marked when the two companies are based in different national cultures.

One vital issue when integrating any acquisition, then, is how to speed the process of getting dozens, hundreds, or thousands of people to work together in harmony. How do you get people from different cultures, who may even have been competitors, to build a new company that will grow and prosper?

From its experience, GE Capital has distilled four steps business leaders can take to bridge the cultural gaps that exist when integrating any acquisition. We have found that failing to take steps like these to address the "soft" side of integration turns the "hard" aspects of integration—such as reconciling different financial-accounting practices—into mechanical exercises that are executed without understanding or finesse, and often without success.

Meet, greet, and plan (urgently). Once the deal is closed and the transfer of ownership becomes official, the GE Capital business leader, with the help of the acquisition manager, organizes orientation and planning sessions for the members of the management team of the new acquisition and their counterparts in GE Capital. The intent is to use these sessions to create a 100-day plan for acquisition integration. These sessions help welcome the new senior managers into GE Capital and give them a chance to socialize with their new colleagues. They also provide an opportunity for both sides to exchange information and share their feelings and reactions about the recently completed deal.

As part of the information exchange, the newly acquired managers are asked to talk about their organization, products, people, and plans. In particular, they are asked to talk about the positive aspects of their company—what they feel good about and what should be built upon. They are then asked to share their thoughts about opportunities for improvement—what could be changed, areas of potential growth, and synergies with GE Capital.

Following that exchange, the GE Capital business leader, the integration manager, and other executives describe what it means to be a part of GE Capital—the values, the responsibilities, the challenges, and the rewards. That includes a presentation and discussion of the standards required of a GE Capital business unit, including a list of approximately 25 policies and practices that need to be incorporated into the way the acquired company does business. Those range from quarterly operating reviews to risk policies to quality and integrity procedures.

Drawing on the standards set by GE Capital and the opportunities for improvement presented by the acquired management team, the group then begins to draft the 100-day plan for acquisition integration. As its name implies, the plan outlines what will be done in the first 100 days to bring the new company into GE Capital. The plan addresses such issues as the need for integrating functions, taking any steps necessary for financial and procedural compliance, making any shifts in compensation and benefits, and managing customer contacts. The 100-day timetable creates a sense of urgency, challenge, and excitement; it imbues the integration with a feeling of zest and energy. At the same time, it forces the management team to move into action and avoid becoming paralyzed by mixed feelings and personal politics.

Communicate, communicate—and then communicate some more. Creating a communication plan during the due diligence and negotiation phases of a transaction so that employees and external parties are informed as soon as a deal is closed is only the first step in an effective communication program. Keeping the communication process going—and making it reach broadly and deeply throughout the organization— requires more than just sharing information bulletins. It requires the creation of forums for dialogue and interaction that can help span the cultural chasm between acquirer and acquiree.

As in any communication plan, there are four considerations: Audience, timing, mode, and message. For example, for one of its integrations, GE Capital's Private Label Credit Card business identified several distinct audiences: the senior managers of both organizations; the integration manager and his team; all of the employees of the acquired organization; all of GE Capital's employees; the customers, clients, and vendors of the combined company; the community; and the media. The appropriate time to communicate was identified for each audience—before the deal was closed, for instance, or at closing, or perhaps 60 days after the closing. And for each audience, the appropriate mode of communication was selected, ranging from newsletters and memos to videos to small-group huddles to town meetings and visits from management.

A fundamental message about GE Capital's culture underlay the entire communication effort—that at GE Capital, communication and involvement are valued and considered to be critical success factors; that GE Capital does not hide information from employees; that GE Capital wants to create a relationship of trust and open dialogue across all boundaries in the organization. That's why managers, and not professional communicators, are asked to take the lead in many aspects of the process—so that they will engage in dialogue with their employees, peers, customers, and others. At another level, messages about the course of the integration process are communicated by disseminating the 100-day plan itself, so that everyone has an opportunity to learn its broad outlines.

The assumption here is that the more people know about what is happening, the more they will be able to accept change and overcome their cultural and historical differences. But in GE Capital's experience, such intensive communication, even when combined with extensive integration planning, is sometimes not enough to bridge deep cultural gaps. A more direct approach to cultural integration may be needed as well.

Address the cultural issues head-on. Several years ago, as GE Capital began to make more acquisitions outside the United States, it became clear that a number of unrecognized cultural issues were getting in the way of fast and effective integration. Those issues were rooted in differences in corporate culture but were magnified and complicated by differences in national culture. For example, in some companies, deference to authority prevented managers from challenging, questioning, and thus enriching GE Capital's ideas about how to grow the new business. In countries with hierarchical social systems, this pattern of deference seemed to be even more apparent. In other settings, seemingly straightforward instructions were misinterpreted, not only because of language barriers but also because of assumptions about intentions. And in still other cases, GE Capital found that newly acquired leaders didn't comfortably accept the autonomy that comes along with empowerment.

It became clear that cultural issues were getting in the way of fast, effective integration.

To deal with those issues, GE Capital worked with a consulting firm to construct a systematic process of cross-cultural analysis, leading up to a structured three-day "cultural workout" session between GE Capital and the newly acquired management team. That process is now applied in most of GE Capital's acquisitions, especially when there is a significant non-U.S. component.

Here is how the process works. Using the results of focus groups and interviews with customers and employees, a computer-generated analysis is developed that plots the acquired company's culture on a scattergram across four dimensions: costs, technology, brands, and customers. The analysis also contrasts how employees see the company with the way customers see it. A similar survey is done for the GE Capital business.

Once the survey results are ready, the managers from both GE Capital and the acquired company meet for the three-day cultural workout. (If everything is on schedule, this meeting takes place at or close to the end of the first 100 days.) At that session, the data from the two companies are compared to highlight areas of convergence and difference. With a facilitator, participants go through the data and talk about why they think the results turned out the way they did. They talk about the history of their companies, the folklore, and the heroes that made them what they are. That leads to focused discussions about cultural differences and similarities and their implications for doing business—for instance, how to go to market, how much to focus on cost, or how concepts of authority differ.

By the third day of the session, participants shift their focus from the past to the future. Based on what has been accomplished in the first 100 days, they are asked two questions: Where do they want to take the company? and What kind of future do they want to create? That discussion results in a written outline of a new business plan for the acquired company, based on the goals that were established as part of the original deal, now augmented by the collective dreams and aspirations of the new management team. After the first 100 days, the stage is set for continuing the integration and development process over the next six months or more on the basis of a shared understanding of cultural differences and a concrete plan for bridging the gaps.

To move from the few to the many, cascade the integration process. Bridging cultural gaps with the acquired management team is critical to the integration process and almost always leads to a richer business plan to which more employees are committed. But in most cases, hundreds or even thousands of other people also need to be part of the process.

A powerful way to integrate cultures is to assign short-term projects to yield quick results.

How can that process of bridging cultures be spread beyond the management team?

The results of the cultural workout can be widely shared and discussed through small-group meetings, videos, and other channels. That gives the wider employee population access to the same body of cultural data as the management team has—and the same opportunity to digest it and consider its implications for the integration. But a more powerful way to spread the cultural integration further is through action. Short-term projects that focus on achieving results quickly and include staff members from both GE Capital and the acquired company almost always serve to bridge the gap between cultures. In other words, the faster people from both companies are given opportunities to work together on important business issues, the faster integration will occur.

For example, in 1995, when GE Capital's Global Consumer Finance business acquired Minebea Financial, a Japanese financial-services company, the business leader commissioned a number of joint GCF-Minebea teams to accomplish critical business goals in the first 100 days. One team reduced the cost of materials through an initiative aimed at having the suppliers manage inventory. Another arranged for the sale of written-off receivables. Still another reduced the time it took to respond to customers' telephone calls from three minutes to ten seconds. As important as those results were, equally important was what the people from GCF and Minebea learned by working together. By achieving results quickly, everybody could immediately see the benefits of the acquisition—that more could be achieved together than could ever have been accomplished separately.

GE Capital also has been experimenting with other ways to help individuals deal with differences in national cultures. For example, an American assigned to lead a key function in India is individually coached by an external consultant who specializes in national cultures. The consultant can help the relocating manager understand in advance subtle, but critical differences in culture—the need for specific, rather than general, instructions, for example, or the importance of variations in attitudes toward class and gender, in the willingness to criticize others, or in the degree to which employees are expected to take initiative.

Finally, to introduce the GE Capital culture to high-potential leaders in those organizations newly acquired from outside the United States, the company has initiated a program called Capital University. In this program, selected middle managers are given 6-to 12-month assignments in a GE Capital business or head-office function in the United States. With their families, these managers learn not only about GE Capital but also about the national culture in which GE Capital is rooted. They, too, are coached individually by consultants about differences in national cultures.

A Work in Progress

For almost a decade, GE Capital's leaders have been thinking about how to make acquisition integration a core competence, and they have engaged hundreds of people in the effort. Starting in 1989, workout teams have mapped out the entire transaction process and have identified essential steps for integration. In 1992, GE Capital employed a "change acceleration" methodology to identify best integration practices and develop a set of model approaches. And since 1995, GE Capital has sponsored periodic conferences to refine those best practices, share tools and lessons, and discuss case studies of integration efforts currently in progress.

Today these lessons are available on-line to all GE Capital business leaders over the company's intranet. There, too, are communication plans, 100-day plans, functional integration checklists, workshop agendas, consulting resources, and the like. A staff member from the corporate human-resources department keeps these materials up-to-date and assists in accessing them.

Despite this progress, acquisition integration remains an ongoing challenge for GE Capital. The structure of every acquisition is unique; each has a one-of-a-kind business strategy; each has its own personality and culture. No matter how many insights and models previous transactions generate, the next deal is always different, as much an art as a science. Therefore, any company that hopes to benefit from GE Capital's experience needs to accept at least one aspect of its culture—that competence is something never fully attained, that it is only the jumping-off point for an ever higher standard. Today, drawing from the lessons it has learned, GE Capital is better at acquisitions than it was last year. But next year, the goal is to be even better.

What It Takes to Be an Integration Manager

INTEGRATION MANAGERS manage the integration process, not the business. To do so, they:

Facilitate and manage integration activities by

- Working closely with the managers of the acquired company to make its practices consistent with GE Capital's requirements and standards.

- Creating strategies to quickly communicate important information about the integration effort to employees.
- Helping the new company add functions that may not have existed before, such as risk management or quality improvement.

Help the acquired business understand GE Capital by

- Assisting managers of the newly acquired company as they navigate through the GE Capital system—explaining to a new finance manager in Taipei, for example, who reports to a business in Chicago, how to buy a personal computer through the GE purchasing network.
- Educating the new management team about GE Capital's business cycle; reviews; and such other processes as strategic planning, budgeting, and human resource assessments.
- Translating and explaining GE's and GE Capital's various acronyms.
- Helping managers of the acquired company understand GE Capital's culture and business customs.
- Helping managers of the acquired company understand both the fundamental and minor changes in their jobs. For example, a CFO accustomed to having full responsibility for tax and treasury accounting needs to be informed that CFOs in the GE Capital system don't usually cover that territory.
- Introducing GE Capital's business practices to the new company, including its "workout," "quality leadership," "change acceleration," and "management-education" programs.

Help GE Capital understand the acquired business by

- Making sure managers of the newly acquired company are not swamped with requests for information from GE

Capital. A number of integration managers insist, for example, that all requests for information go through them so that they can sort through the important ones and allow the other managers to stay focused on the business.

- Briefing GE executives about the newly acquired company to help them understand why it works the way it does.

Originally published in January–February 1998
Reprint 98101

Integration Managers

Special Leaders for Special Times

RONALD N. ASHKENAS AND

SUZANNE C. FRANCIS

Executive Summary

ALTHOUGH THE INTEGRATION OF an acquired company with the parent organization is a delicate and complicated process, traditionally no one has ever been responsible for that process—for charting how the two companies will combine their operations, for seeing to it that the integration project meets its deadlines and performance targets, and for educating the new people about the parent company and vice versa.

Some enlightened companies have recognized this gap and have appointed a guide—the integration manager—to shepherd everyone through the rocky territory that two organizations must cross before they can function effectively together. The authors have interviewed a number of these leaders in depth, as well as some of the people with whom they've worked. They've determined that integration managers help the merger process in four principal ways: they speed it up, create a structure for it, forge social connections between the two organizations, and help engineer short-term successes.

In this article, the authors detail five acquisitions—at TI, General Cable, Meritor Automotive, Lucent, and Johnson & Johnson—and discuss the role that integration managers played in each. They describe exactly what sort of person should do this job. The integration manager must be able to jump into complex situations quickly, relate to many levels of authority smoothly, and bridge gaps in culture and perception.

The ever-changing organizations of the Internet age will need leaders with similar skills. In fact, the authors contend, the integration manager should be considered a prototype for the leader of the future.

CONSIDER THE IRONY: less than half of all mergers and acquisitions ever reach their promised strategic and financial goals, yet companies spent more on M&A last year than ever before. According to investment bankers J.P. Morgan, companies worldwide spent $3.3 trillion on mergers and acquisitions in 1999—fully 32% more than was spent in 1998. Basically, that means those companies failed to get the value they expected from a whopping $1.6 trillion in investments. That's a very expensive irony indeed.

Even more ironic: although the integration of an acquired company with the parent organization is a delicate and complicated process, traditionally no one has ever been responsible for that process. The due-diligence team develops a deep knowledge of the acquired company, but that team usually disbands after the deal closes. A management team will eventually run the merged organization, but often no one is responsible for the integration process itself—for charting how the two companies will combine their operations, for seeing to it that the integration meets its deadlines and performance targets, for educating the new people about the parent company, and vice versa.

To counter this gap in accountability, some enlightened companies have appointed a guide—the integration manager—to shepherd everyone through the rocky and often uncharted territory that two organizations must cross before they can function as one. Guiding this kind of expedition takes a new type of leader, someone who can jump into complex situations quickly, relate to many levels of authority smoothly, and bridge gaps in culture and perception. But this leader also needs some traditional organizational strengths such as world-class project management skills, a deep understanding of the parent company, and enough clout to be effective.

We first encountered these new leaders at GE Capital. And since 1998, when we took a close look at how integration managers worked—as we described in our article written with Lawrence J. DeMonaco, "Making the Deal Real: How GE Capital Integrates Acquisitions" (Chapter 7)—several other companies have formally designated such leaders. We have interviewed a number of them in depth, as well as some of the people with whom they've worked. Even though the acquisitions we examined covered a range of industries, geographies, and transaction sizes, the common themes are striking.

We found that integration managers help the process in four principal ways: they speed it up, create a structure for it, forge social connections between the two organizations, and help engineer short-term successes that produce business results. To show how they work, we will tell you about five acquisitions and the role integration managers played in each. Then we'll look at exactly what sort of person should do this job.

A Job Waiting to Be Defined

In July 1998, when Bill Quinn was asked to become Johnson & Johnson's first-ever integration manager for its $3.7 billion acquisition of DePuy Incorporated, he was puzzled about the role he was being asked to play. DePuy was one of the world's leading orthopedic medical device companies; with 3,000 employees, 15 manufacturing facilities, and worldwide product sales, it was much larger than J&J's own orthopedic device unit, with which it would be combined. So even though the newly consolidated company would report to J&J's worldwide chairman for medical devices, the top business leaders would be the current DePuy executives.

As the head of J&J's Quality Institute and an 18-year veteran of the company, Quinn had a firm grasp of J&J's business processes and how to go about improving them. But what was required here? Who was acquiring whom? What did integration really mean in this case? And how would Quinn fit in?

In many ways, the role of the integration manager is more akin to an entrepreneurial job in a start-up company than to a position in an established organization. Like a start-up, an acquisition begins with a strategy and a financial plan that embody a bright idea of what a new organization will be in the future. But those theoretical plans have to become reality; they are often transformed as the organization strives to quickly realize value from the money invested. The roles of the people involved—

and the way they will relate to one another to make this happen—usually aren't well defined.

Often, then, the first challenge for an integration manager is to define his or her job. Quinn spent a hair-raisingly intense two weeks coming up to speed. He interviewed the key DePuy and J&J executives involved in the deal. He talked to managers from J&J's past few acquisitions. Quinn read everything possible about the industry and the acquisition. He consulted the business development people who had worked on the deal. He met with at least a half-dozen consulting firms, each of which offered its own perspective on how the integration should be handled.

Quickly, a role began to take shape in his mind. If his job was to manage the process, Quinn thought, he needed to be viewed as powerful—but also impartial—by people from both organizations. That suggested he should play the role of consultant—but one with privileged access to the top executives who would be in charge of the new organization. He gained that by joining the integration steering committee, on which sat the two DePuy executives who would eventually run the new organization; the head of the original J&J orthopedic device unit; and the new organization's boss, J&J group operating chairman Jim Lenehan.

Indeed, Quinn concluded, he needed even more access to Lenehan than membership on the integration committee afforded. That didn't necessarily mean that he should be reporting directly to Lenehan. In fact, the reporting relationship never was announced or clarified. The important thing was that people throughout Johnson & Johnson and DePuy knew that Quinn could go to Lenehan at any point and therefore took him seriously enough to seek him out.

As the integration progressed, Quinn's original thinking was confirmed. But two other roles emerged that he hadn't anticipated. The first surprise was that Quinn turned out to be a lightning rod for many people's emotions. "Everyone was under such extreme pressure and emotional stress," he explains. "They wanted to make sure the right thing was done. They did not want to see people get hurt. Many times, I was the one place where they could let that stress out. There was one day in particular when I spent four hours on the phone, and most of the time people were yelling. I was taking it really hard. Then the lightbulb went on and I realized their frustration was not directed at me. Then it was a lot easier."

The second surprise was that having access to J&J's group operating chairman was a two-way street. It gave him clout with others, but people expected him to use that clout to raise important questions with Lenehan and the integration steering committee when they thought a decision might be going the wrong way. Some executives from both DePuy and J&J were reluctant at times to push back on the steering committee, either because they were new to the organization or because they were trying to establish themselves as part of the new team. Quinn was perceived to be in a better position to advocate a contrary view since he did not have a vested interest. But to do so took courage and persistence because, as Quinn explains, "The dilemma is doing what you think is right for the business versus doing what is easier to sell at the moment. In one case, it took me three attempts to shift their thinking on an important decision. At times, it was pretty uncomfortable coming back to them—as if I didn't understand the word no. It would have been really easy to drop it."

That courage was well rewarded: with Quinn's help, the new business came together with less conflict than J&J had experienced in some of its previous integrations, J&J retained the people it had wanted to keep, and the acquisition met its strategic and financial targets. In fact, J&J's top managers consider the DePuy acquisition to be one of its most successful, and exactly a year after that project started, they asked Quinn to manage an even bigger acquisition for the company.

All of the integration managers we interviewed had experiences similar to Bill Quinn's in that they started their assignments with a sketchy and ambiguous job description, which they filled in over time.

Life on Fast-Forward

There are two critical periods in the life of most acquisitions. The first is the time between the deal's announcement and its close. The second is the first 100 days after the close. One of the integration manager's most important roles is to move everyone as quickly as possible through those two deadlines.

That's what Jodi Mahon did when, in April 1999, she was named integration manager for General Cable's acquisition of BICC's $1.8 billion worldwide energy-cable and cable-systems businesses. Her mandate was clear: move the integration process forward as fast as possible so the new company could get a running start the day after the deal's close—in just six weeks.

At $1.2 billion, the parent company was slightly smaller than its acquisition. Together, they would form a $3 billion organization that would be third in its industry. Mahon brought seven years of company experience to the integration manager role, and she had been a member of the business development team that put the deal together. So part of her job was straightforward— working with an integration team to identify the critical elements that needed to be in place by day one. Those critical pieces were as basic as what the newly combined company would be called (BICC General) and as challenging as what the management and reporting structure would be.

But even though identifying what needed to be in place was straightforward, making it happen was not. The management team had not finalized its thinking on many issues, including the structure of several business units and the candidates for some leadership assignments. What's more, Mahon recalls, "we had a culture clash with the people within the businesses we acquired. We operated at a warp-speed faster than they did. We focused and managed our business totally differently."

Mahon's main job for the first six weeks was to push through this maze of uncertainty in time for the close date. She was not the final decision maker on many issues, but without her involvement many decisions would still have lingered beyond the close date. Even worse, they would have been decided unilaterally by the CEO. Mahon saw her role as one of anticipating and then heading off potential disaster, like an air traffic controller. "You see things that are coming," she explains. "If people cannot come to an agreement, you have to force them into a room and say, 'Make a call on this.' "

Once the acquisition is officially closed, the need for speed remains, or even accelerates. One of BICC General's main goals in the first 100 days, for example, was to achieve a $12 million annualized cost savings from its North American operations. The senior executive team mapped out exactly where the savings would come from and divvied up that number among the various functions and business units. Mahon's job was to focus the leadership team on those numbers despite all the distractions of other issues and challenges. "I moved around like a cop and said to people, 'I'm going to arrest you if you don't get this done by next Tuesday,' " she recalls.

Thanks in large part to her facilitation, the North American operations exceeded its $12 million cost-reduction goal in that first 100 days. And based on that success, the company decided to accelerate its systems integration work. By the end of 1999, just six months after the deal had closed, General Cable and BICC's former North American operations had become a fully integrated company.

Putting the Chaos in Order

Putting two companies together requires disconnecting and reconnecting hundreds of processes and procedures as quickly as possible. Clearly it's a team sport, and, obviously, well-organized teams will do better than uncoordinated ones. So one of the most effective ways an integration manager guides the process is by creating the structure within which the team can operate effectively. That requires the most traditional of project management skills.

Witness what Ernie Rodriguez did when Lucent Technologies bought Ascend Communications in 1999. At nearly $20 billion when the deal was announced in January, it was one of the largest technology mergers in U.S. history. From it, Lucent expected to gain talented people and critical products—and something more. Parts of Lucent would be blended into Ascend to form Lucent's InterNetworking business. The new unit would be

headed by Ascend executives who could not be brought
on board until the deal was officially closed. But Lucent
CEO Rich McGinn was not about to wait that long to
begin the integration process. So he asked Rodriguez, a
senior executive with 30 years experience at Lucent and
Bell Labs, to be the integration manager just before the
deal was announced. Rodriguez would pave the way for
the new management team.

Rodriguez had a reputation for simplifying complicated situations. Shortly after the deal was announced,
he created a road map to help people see the work ahead
in a logical and achievable way. Since one of the ultimate
goals was to introduce Ascend's corporate organization
and its looser Silicon Valley–Route 128 culture into
Lucent, Rodriguez set up teams of people drawn from
both organizations. The teams were tailored to address
the four key issues for this integration: customers, product solutions, people, and administration. Each team had
two leaders—one from Lucent and one from Ascend.

Rodriguez united the teams by instituting common
tools, measures, and project management disciplines.
And he did one seemingly small thing that had a big uni-
fying effect. The teams' mandate was to have as many
systems up and running as possible on the day the deal
closed. But, Rodriguez explains, "with all the government
and stockholder approvals required, we couldn't predict
when that date might occur." To sweep away that uncertainty and focus everyone on the same point, Rodriguez
set a date and *created* some certainty. "Let's assume that
the deal will close on April 30," he said. "What do we
want to do by then?"

The groups set expectations for what they thought
should be done by April 30—day one for the merged
company. To test the integration, they worked up sce-

narios for daily business events. Could a customer, for example, place an order for an Ascend product sold in Europe on April 30? Could a new employee be hired smoothly? They tested the work that had been done against these scenarios in a "ready to merge" meeting in early April. This work made it easy for everyone to see—and agree—that they would be integrated satisfactorily in some areas by the closing but would need to do more work in other areas.

Knowing now exactly what they had to do, the teams focused on getting the remaining systems up and running by the actual close date, which turned out to be in June. After the close, they continued through October, working on the systems—such as pricing, the quote-to-cash process, and customer support—that could not be done before the deal was closed.

By late summer 1999, with the management team of the newly merged entity well in place, Rodriguez had handed over the daily responsibilities for integration to the business unit president. He then moved on to his next assignment—integration manager for Lucent's International Network Services acquisition, which had been recently announced.

Building the Social Connections

The people involved in mergers and acquisitions are often strangers, thrown together in a joint enterprise, sometimes against their will. Besides keeping the day-to-day business going, employees at both companies need to build new relationships, which often involves bridging language and culture gaps. The integration manager can clear paths between the two cultures by facilitating the social connections among people on both sides.

This was an important part of what Brian Bonner did when Texas Instruments asked him to be the integration manager for its $1.3 billion acquisition of Unitrode, a Merrimack, New Hampshire, maker of analog signal-processing products. The goal was to integrate Unitrode into TI's Advanced Analog Products business, so Unitrode's people needed to understand and adopt all of TI's key business and HR processes. But the strategic value of the acquisition, Bonner realized, lay not only in Unitrode's products, patents, and facilities but also in its talented and experienced workforce—particularly its analog engineers. Bonner needed to find a way to integrate them into TI without alienating them.

TI had already established standardized processes for connecting relatively generic systems such as purchasing, facilities, security, and telecommunications before the closing date. It was Bonner's first job, then, to identify the right senior people from both TI and Unitrode to look at the larger strategic issues: revenue goals, brand strategies, and product development, for instance. This was a task that required subtlety.

Much of what makes integration managers valuable is the fact that they have room to maneuver where others, more fixed in their roles in both companies, do not.

"Unitrode was a successful, mature, complex business, not a dot-com start-up," Bonner explains, "so it was important to match the right levels of TI experience and knowledge with those of the Unitrode leaders." An 18-year veteran of TI, Bonner had developed personal relationships with legions of people whom he felt comfortable calling on to get involved or to provide support.

Much of what makes integration managers valuable is the fact that they have room to maneuver where others, more fixed in their roles in both companies, do not. By shuttling freely up and down the organizational hierarchy, in and out of different departments and companies, and across different locations, they can make things happen that would not have happened otherwise.

This was literally true for Bonner, since the TI executives on the teams were in Texas and their Unitrode counterparts were in New Hampshire. As Bonner shuttled back and forth between Dallas and Merrimack, he found himself picking up on problems that no one else was in a position to see. He began to leave room in his days for one-on-one meetings, particularly with the Unitrode team members in New Hampshire. In those meetings, he found, "I was talking about really important issues that hadn't come up before. It was a chance to correct misconceptions, coach people on how to handle problems, learn more about how products were developed or manufactured, and understand the Unitrode ways of doing things that should be tried at TI."

People throughout Unitrode were concerned about having a new boss and playing by unfamiliar rules in a large corporation. How could they be heard? Recognizing that no amount of long-distance teleconferencing technology was going to allay such fears, Bonner held a series of face-to-face focus groups for Unitrode employees, so they could see—physically see—that he and TI would actually listen to their concerns. Once those concerns were aired, he could begin translating TI-speak into their terms.

"Even though up in New Hampshire they speak English like they do in Texas," Bonner says, "we noticed that our vocabularies were different. We described things in TI-speak, and they would listen to it and interpret it with the filter they had from their language." For instance, TI executives would talk about developing product strategies, and the Unitrode people would tune out, assuming that was no longer their responsibility. TI, though, still wanted the Unitrode people to develop their own product strategies and submit them for approval through the TI structure. It was only through face-to-face discussions with Bonner and others that such misconceptions were discovered and assuaged.

Time and again, Bonner had to anticipate the social connections that would be necessary to support the integration. This wasn't his only responsibility; it wasn't his highest priority. But those connections were essential for bringing together two very different businesses whose success depended on their being tightly coupled functionally while maintaining unique cultures in separate locations.

Getting Early Results

Speeding things along, building structures, and forging social connections are critical but, taken by themselves, they are like having a map but never using it to go anywhere. Until the journey leads to business results, the deal does not pay off. Thus the fourth task for integration managers is to orchestrate tangible successes rapidly that could not have been achieved before the companies came together. Such successes—generally achieved within the first 100 days—not only start to pay for the deal but also build confidence in the minds of managers and staff that the acquisition makes sense. That confidence is often a necessary prerequisite to true integration.

Consider Meritor Automotive (now ArvinMeritor). When the company bought Volvo's heavy-vehicle axle plant in Lindesberg, Sweden, in October 1998, the integration challenge was as much psychological and cultural as it was operational. Since its construction, the Lindesberg facility had been an integral member of the Volvo family. While certainly not inefficient, the plant was focused on guaranteeing reliability for Volvo's heavy-vehicle assembly operations, not on cost. Consequently, the plant was vertically integrated, producing all its own axle components, and it had a history of making extra investments in staffing and equipment.

When the plant became part of Meritor, it became part of Meritor's global manufacturing system, which meant it would need to outsource the production of non-core components that it used to make itself. It also meant that Volvo became a customer—and not the only one. These two changes required a huge shift in mindset. To help Lindesberg achieve it, Meritor assigned Dave Dernberger, a 27-year veteran of the company, as on-site integration manager.

In the first week after the deal officially closed, he organized an integration workshop for the Swedish management team and key Meritor people. One of its aims was to launch several projects that could achieve business results in 100 days or less. Given the skepticism of the Swedish managers about being part of Meritor, Dernberger felt that these successes would be critical in getting them (and everyone else) on board.

The workshop identified ten high-priority initiatives that would demonstrate the benefits of being part of the Meritor global supply system and that would make a real difference to the bottom line in the first year. One of the projects involved outsourcing a specific component—

something new to Lindesberg's management and staff, who had never created a spec sheet, solicited bids, or developed an outsourcing contract. Another project was aimed at marketing some of Lindesberg's unique heat-treating capabilities to other Meritor plants.

One by one, the Lindesberg plant completed the ten projects. The result was not only the achievement of its operational goals but also the true beginnings of a shift in mind-set. For example, Dernberger says, "the previous owner, now our customer, still expected that he could call the plant and request engineering changes, just like before. Now our people say, 'There may be a cost issue here or an impact on other customers that we must consider.'"

These initial, relatively small, successes gave Lindesberg's staff the confidence to take on more ambitious projects with Meritor's global European manufacturing system. Within just a single year, the Lindesberg plant became a fully integrated part of the Meritor system.

Who Can Do This Job?

It's obvious from the five cases we've just described that it takes a special combination of skills to be an effective integration manager. (See "What Integration Managers Do" at the end of this article.) The leaders who can fill this role are not easily found in the corporate phone book. From our research and direct experience with integration managers, we have seen five likely predictors of success for individuals in this role.

DEEP KNOWLEDGE OF THE ACQUIRING COMPANY

Managers joining a new company need to ask the integration manager how to prepare reports, where to get information, how to handle a customer request, how much data are needed to back up a conclusion, whom to talk to about various subjects, and more. They need to be coached through the company's informal measures of success by someone who knows them thoroughly. Integration managers need to understand and articulate their own company's culture. And they need an industrial-size Rolodex—ready access to the key people in their company whom newly acquired managers need to contact.

We are often asked whether an integration manager can come from the newly acquired company. The answer is a categorical no. It is impossible for someone from the acquired side of the deal to know enough about the parent company's formal and informal expectations for the merger and for managers. That takes a veteran who has been through the wars and has seen, firsthand, what success is all about. So it's not surprising that all the integration managers whose stories we have told in this article were longtime employees who had held a wide variety of line and staff positions, moving through different business units, functions, and geographic locations. That being said, we have seen several cases in which a counterpart from the acquired company acted as a partner with the integration manager.

NO NEED FOR CREDIT

Sometimes, an integration manager needs to be tough and unbending with managers and staff, particularly about deadlines or about coming to a decision. But other times, the integration manager needs to be an empathetic listener—not only with employees whose jobs are affected but also with senior executives who might be frustrated, exhausted, anxious, or angry. Not everyone can flip between being tough and being supportive. And not everyone can do that with people at different levels up and down an organization. A good integration manager knows which style is appropriate in which situation. Some of this flexibility is innate, but some of it can only be developed over time. That's another reason why most integration managers are veterans of their organizations.

Yet even experience and personal skill are not enough. In the final analysis, a major generator of this kind of flexibility is deep self-confidence combined with relatively few ego requirements. The integration manager cannot be concerned with getting credit—or even recognition—for an effective integration. As TI's Brian Bonner notes: "The danger of being the integration manager is that you think you are the CEO of this deal and you are not. You are just there to get this job done and move on." Credit belongs to the executives, managers, and staff.

COMFORT WITH CHAOS

Every integration manager we've seen had to mobilize dozens or even hundreds of people in numerous teams that cross functions, organizations, cultures, and geographies. And that takes exquisite project management and organizational skills. The teams need clear assignments; common formats for their outputs; disciplined timelines; and coordinated meeting schedules, meeting formats, communication mechanisms, and review processes. The integration

It's virtually impossible to disconnect and reconnect two companies completely and perfectly from the start. So an integration manager cannot be wedded to perfection or bound by rigid project management tools.

manager needs not only to put this machinery and structure into place but also to coordinate and manage it on an ongoing basis.

Managing an integration project, however, is not entirely the same as managing a traditional project. It requires some tempering of the usual engineering-control mentality, for two reasons. First, unlike most project management assignments, team leaders and members in an acquisition integration project generally do not work directly for the integration manager. In fact, until all the organizational structures are clarified, some people who work on integration teams may not know to whom they report, or even whether they will have jobs or bosses in the new organization. So the integration manager needs to motivate and involve people not only by working through established channels of authority but also by inspiring people to become committed to the new organization and by making the process itself exciting.

Second, unlike many traditional projects, it's virtually impossible to disconnect and reconnect two companies completely and perfectly from the start. So an integration manager cannot be wedded to perfection or bound by rigid project management tools or control mechanisms. Meritor's Dave Dernberger, for instance, found that at one point he had to literally throw away his project management software and rely instead on a large wall chart dotted with hundreds of Post-it notes, which he and the team leaders in Lindesberg could move around almost daily. More traditional project managers might want to freeze the design of the integration once it's in place. The best integration managers keep the process moving by constantly recalibrating their plans.

A RESPONSIBLE INDEPENDENCE

As in any expedition, the guides leading acquisition integration projects do not hang up their hats at five o'clock and go home for the night. Anyone who takes on the role needs to be prepared for six to eight months of intense activity that can consume almost every waking hour. As J&J's Bill Quinn said when asked about the advice he would give to a newly appointed integration manager: "Take your spouse out tonight, because you are not going to get a chance to do it again for a number of months. Then put on your running shoes, because you're going to need them!" But the long and intense hours are only half the story. The real issue is that those long hours are almost totally unsupervised in the traditional sense. Day to day, no one is going to tell the integration manager what to do, where to focus, whom to contact, or how to add value. Anyone selected for the job needs to be able to take initiative and make independent judgments. But that individual also needs to know when to check in with the right people to make sure things are moving in the right direction. This makes it vitally important that the integration manager have—or win—the trust of the most senior executives in his or her company.

EMOTIONAL AND CULTURAL INTELLIGENCE

There's a saying in the acquisitions world that integrations would be easy if no people were involved. And unfortunately, too many organizations fail because they treat the integration of acquired companies just that way—as an engineering exercise and not as one that affects people's lives and futures. To avoid this blunder, it is critical to select an integration manager who can appreciate the emotional and cultural issues involved, handle them personally, and help others deal with them constructively. This is particularly important in situations where the business leaders and the business development people who have spearheaded the acquisition are heavily driven by financial and strategic considerations; those leaders tend to give the people side of the equation less weight. In such cases—and in our view, this is most of the time—the integration manager provides a critical counterbalance. The key word here is "balance." Integration activities can't be allowed to degenerate into gripe sessions or personal lobbying. Nor can they be allowed to slow down work. Effective integration managers create opportunities for people to vent their feelings but then help employees move on.

A New Leader for the Internet Economy

We have focused here on managing the integration of acquired companies. But the kind of leadership we've been describing has wider implications. Organizations in the Internet age are constantly reinventing themselves, creating flexible and boundaryless structures, and building and reworking partnerships and alliances. Most senior leaders in these ever-changing businesses will not be hierarchical strategists and order givers with permanent, multiyear assignments. More often than not, they will be consultants, facilitators, communicators, project managers, and bridge builders, asked to move in and out of situations at a moment's notice. (See "Where Are They Now?" at the end of this article.) Many will need skills very similar to the ones an integration manager needs.

In the final analysis, integration managers may represent the manager of the future—not just in what they do but in how they do it. These leaders not only drive change, they are subject to change. They help a newly formed organization succeed while at the same time learning how to be personally successful.

The individuals portrayed in this article are by no means perfect and complete examples of this new kind of role. They all struggled with aspects of the job and speculated that they would do some things differently the second time around. But it is this ability to reflect and learn that also made them successful in the first round. In the Internet age, in which organizations change at the speed of light, this ability to learn and adjust constantly may be the difference between the organizations that succeed and those that don't.

What Integration Managers Do

Every acquisition is different, demanding a different balance of efforts from the integration manager. But in a single integration project, the manager may use any or all of the following four strategies.

Inject Speed

- Ramp up planning efforts
- Accelerate implementation
- Push for decisions and actions
- Monitor progress against goals, and pace the integration efforts to meet deadlines

Engineer Success

- Help identify critical business synergies
- Launch 100-day projects to achieve short-term bottom-line results

- Orchestrate transfers of best practices between companies

Make Social Connections

- Act as traveling ambassador between locations and businesses

- Serve as a lighting rod for hot issues; allow employees to vent

- Interpret the customs, language, and cultures of both companies

Create Structure

- Provide flexible integration frameworks

- Mobilize joint teams

- Create key events and timelines

- Facilitate team and executive reviews

Where Are They Now?

THE INTEGRATION MANAGER'S JOB is necessarily temporary, based on the immediate needs of the organization. Often, there's no guaranteed next assignment for the integration manager or no definite plan for fitting that individual back into the organization. Of the five integration managers in this article, two returned to their original jobs and three took broader roles in their organizations. Here's what happened.

- *Texas Instruments's Brian Bonner* served as integration manager for TI's Power Trends acquisition, which started in October 1999; was named TI's CIO in January 2000.

- **ArvinMeritor's Dave Dernberger** continues to work at ArvinMeritor's Lindesberg, Sweden, location, but has assumed responsibilities for Pan-European operations.

- **BICC General's Jodi Mahon** returned to her previous position as head of business development at BICC General.

- **Johnson & Johnson's Bill Quinn** served as integration manager for J&J's $4.9 billion Centocor biotechnology acquisition, which was announced in July 1999, and then returned to his previous position as head of J&J's Quality Institute.

- **Lucent's Ernie Rodriguez** served as integration manager for Lucent's $3.7 billion acquisition of International Network Services; returned to his previous role as the vice president of advanced technologies at Bell Laboratories, Lucent's research group.

Originally published in November–December 2000
Reprint R00604

About the Contributors

At the time this article was originally published, **ROBERT AIELLO** was a managing director and cohead of the Technology Mergers and Acquisitions Group at Prudential Securities in New York City.

RONALD N. ASHKENAS is Managing Partner of Robert H. Schaffer & Associates and an internationally recognized consultant and speaker on organizational change and transformation. In addition to his work in the area of acquisition integration, Mr. Ashkenas also coaches CEOs and senior executive teams on how to strengthen their organization's performance while building managerial capability. He is the coauthor of three *Harvard Business Review* articles and the author of dozens of other articles and book chapters. He also is the senior author of *The Boundaryless Organization* and its companion field guide. He can be reached by e-mail at ron@rhsa.com.

DENNIS CAREY is Vice Chairman of Spencer Stuart U.S., and co-Managing Director of the U.S. Board Services Practice. He specializes in the recruitment of corporate directors and CEOs of major U.S. corporations. He is also a member of the firm's High Technology Practice. As founder of the M&A Group, an organization he cochairs with the CEOs of Tyco International Ltd. and SmithKline Beecham PLC, he has facilitated the introduction of early stage companies with venture capitalists, investment banks, and major strategic relation-

205

ships and partners for companies in the broadband/telecom-
munications and IT arenas. In addition to his work with the
M&A Group, he is cofounder of The Director's Institute at
The Wharton School, serves as a director at several publicly
traded companies, is an arbitrator with the American Arbitra-
tion Association, and serves on the editorial advisory board of
Directors and Boards Magazine. Mr. Carey has authored
numerous articles on governance, CEO succession, and business strategy that have appeared in recent editions of the
*McKinsey Quarterly, Directors and Boards Magazine, Chal-
lenge—The Magazine of Economic Affairs*, the *Wall Street
Journal*, and the *New York Times*. His book *CEO Succession*
was published by Oxford University Press in 2000.

SARAH CLIFFE, former Editor of *Sloan Management Review*,
is an Executive Editor of *Harvard Business Review*.

A Vietnam war veteran, **LAWRENCE J. DEMONACO** has
worked with General Electric for over 30 years. His career
with GE has spanned a variety of different roles including
labor relations, content expert for GE's national union negotiations, organization and staffing manager, employee relations
manager, and Vice President of Human Resources at GE Capital. In addition to his human resources leadership roles, Larry
has worked on over 100 acquisitions around the world. In
1998, he coauthored an article on acquisition integration for
Harvard Business Review.

ROBERT G. ECCLES is Founder and President of Advisory
Capital Partners, Inc. (ACP). Prior to starting ACP, Dr. Eccles
was a professor at Harvard Business School and Chairman of
the Organizational Behavior and Human Resource Management areas. He is one of the country's leading experts in performance measurement and reporting, organizational design,

and change. For the past two years he has been an advisor to PricewaterhouseCoopers on their ValueReporting initiative concerning how companies can most effectively communicate with the capital markets. Dr. Eccles has also led a global research project for PricewaterhouseCoopers on how to most effectively use mergers and acquisitions to implement a growth strategy.

SUZANNE C. FRANCIS, Managing Partner of Robert H. Schaffer & Associates, is a well-known speaker and consultant in the area of acquisition integration and has written numerous articles and participated in several studies on integrating acquisitions. She works with clients on major results-producing change efforts and is currently helping a number of corporations that are "frequent acquirers" to develop practical, flexible, and replicable processes for integrating mergers and acquisitions successfully. Before joining RHS&A, Suzanne worked for Xerox Corporation. She can be reached by e-mail at scf@rhsa.com.

KERSTEN L. LANES is Partner in PricewaterhouseCoopers' Management Consulting Services (MCS). She is responsible for MCS's digital marketing activities, including the consulting practice's Web site, portal initiatives, and other on-line and WAP applications. Prior to this role she was responsible for the firm's U.S. Center of Excellence in Strategic Mergers and Acquisitions, advising clients on merger and divestiture strategies, and developing original research. She began her PricewaterhouseCoopers career in the Strategic Change practice, advising financial institutions on strategic planning, market entry strategies, global organization structures, and cost effectiveness programs.

DAVID A. LIGHT is Associate Editor at *Harvard Business Review*. He has been with the *Review* since 1995.

ALFRED RAPPAPORT is the Leonard Spacek Professor Emeritus at Northwestern University's J.L. Kellogg Graduate School of Management where he was a member of the faculty for 28 years. He is also Shareholder Value Advisor to L.E.K. Consulting and author of the widely acclaimed book, *Creating Shareholder Value: The New Standard for Business Performance*. Dr. Rappaport is the author of over 70 articles focusing primarily on applying shareholder value methodology to planning, performance evaluation, incentive compensation, mergers and acquisitions, and corporate governance issues. He has been a guest columnist for the *Wall Street Journal*, the *New York Times*, and *Business Week*. He also created and designed the *Wall Street Journal Shareholder Scoreboard*, a ranking by total shareholder returns of the 1,000 most valuable U.S. corporations, which is published annually.

MARK L. SIROWER is Senior Adviser with The Boston Consulting Group in New York and a Visiting Professor of Mergers and Acquisitions at New York University's Stern School of Business. He is an internationally recognized expert on mergers and acquisitions and post-merger integration issues and his research and writings have been featured in *Business Week*, *Fortune*, *Forbes*, the *Wall Street Journal*, the *New York Times*, *The Economist*, *Financial Times*, *CFO*, and *Barron's*. He is the author of the bestseller *The Synergy Trap: How Companies Lose the Acquisition Game* and speaks worldwide on growing profitably through mergers and acquisitions. Prior to joining BCG he held faculty positions at The Wharton School and Columbia University.

MICHAEL D. WATKINS is Associate Professor of Business Administration at Harvard Business School. He is also a member of the faculty of the Program on Negotiation at Harvard Law School where he teaches negotiation in Senior Executive Program. Prior to joining Harvard Business School, Professor

Watkins was Associate Professor of Public Policy at Harvard University's Kennedy School of Government, where he taught negotiation and persuasion and did research on international diplomacy and the management of organizational transformation. His current research focuses on complex negotiations and organizational transformation, exploring how leaders negotiate and negotiators lead. He is the coauthor of *Right From the Start: Taking Charge in a New Leadership Role.*

THOMAS C. WILSON is Senior Corporate Finance Partner at PricewaterhouseCoopers in London. He specializes in mergers and acquisitions and, in particular, linking the firm's extensive post-closing integration expertise into the front-end value assessment of mergers and acquisition transactions contemplated by clients.

Index